TRANSFORMATION OF
SHUNDE CITY
Pioneer of China's Greater Bay Area

TRANSFORMATION OF SHUNDE CITY

Pioneer of China's Greater Bay Area

Editor

Henry Hing Lee Chan

NEW JERSEY • LONDON • SINGAPORE • BEIJING • SHANGHAI • HONG KONG • TAIPEI • CHENNAI • TOKYO

Published by

World Scientific Publishing Co. Pte. Ltd.
5 Toh Tuck Link, Singapore 596224
USA office: 27 Warren Street, Suite 401-402, Hackensack, NJ 07601
UK office: 57 Shelton Street, Covent Garden, London WC2H 9HE

British Library Cataloguing-in-Publication Data
A catalogue record for this book is available from the British Library.

TRANSFORMATION OF SHUNDE CITY
Pioneer of China's Greater Bay Area

Copyright © 2020 by World Scientific Publishing Co. Pte. Ltd.

All rights reserved. This book, or parts thereof, may not be reproduced in any form or by any means, electronic or mechanical, including photocopying, recording or any information storage and retrieval system now known or to be invented, without written permission from the publisher.

For photocopying of material in this volume, please pay a copying fee through the Copyright Clearance Center, Inc., 222 Rosewood Drive, Danvers, MA 01923, USA. In this case permission to photocopy is not required from the publisher.

ISBN 978-981-121-305-2

For any available supplementary material, please visit
https://www.worldscientific.com/worldscibooks/10.1142/11632#t=suppl

Desk Editor: Lixi Dong

About the Editor

Dr Henry Hing Lee Chan is a Visiting Senior Research Fellow at Cambodia Institute for Cooperation and Peace and Adjunct Research Fellow at Integrated Development Studies Institute, Manila. He completed his BS Electrical Engineering from the University of the Philippines, MSc Biopharmaceutical from University of New South Wales and PhD General Management from Singapore Management University.

Dr Chan is a retired businessman turned academic researcher. His business experience covers banking, real estate, hotel, manufacturing, agriculture and power. He is a versatile researcher working in various disciplines and an active writer and conference and seminar speaker.

He is currently researching on the Chinese economy, Chinese financial sector reform, Chinese SOE reform, ASEAN and Singapore economy, international trading system, US economy, Sino-American trade war, technology and economic growth, Belt & Road Initiative and cross-Strait issue.

He is an op-ed writer for IPP Review, China Daily, The China Watch and The Manila Times. He also writes for Asia Pacific Tech Monitor of Asian & Pacific Centre for Transfer of Technology (APCTT) of the United Nations Economic and Social Commission for Asia and the Pacific (UNESCAP). His current project is a book on Industrial Revolution & Economic Development.

Contents

About the Editor v
Introduction ix

Part 1   Shunde Today   **1**

Chapter 1   Shunde: A General Introduction   3

Chapter 2   Shunde's Lingnan Culture   17

Chapter 3   Shunde's Cultural Life   25

Chapter 4   Shunde's Culinary Culture and Food Industry   39

Chapter 5   Shunde's Celebrities   49

Part 2   Deciphering Shunde's Success: Reform & Innovation   **57**

Chapter 6   The Shunde Economic Phenomenon   59

Chapter 7   Shunde and the World Economy   69

Chapter 8   Shunde's Innovations   81

Chapter 9   Shunde's Successful Reforms   95

Chapter 10   Shunde's Emerging Industries   105

Chapter 11   Shunde's Industrial Parks and the Sino-German Industrial Services Zone   117

Chapter 12 Shunde's Business Environment	129
Chapter 13 Prominent Companies from Shunde	139

Part 3 Holistic Approach to Development: Social Reform Complements Economic Growth — **151**

Chapter 14 Shunde's City Governance	153
Chapter 15 Urbanisation in Shunde	165
Chapter 16 Shunde's Talent Management	175
Chapter 17 Shunde's Education System	183

Part 4 Future of Shunde in the Changing World — **197**

Chapter 18 Shunde's Future	199

Introduction

The papers in these collections were published online at IPP Review over a few months in 2019 with an exceptionally high readership count. The transformation of Shunde, from a historically agricultural county to a bustling manufacturing hub cum liveable city in the past 41 year since the reform and opening up of China in 1978, has captured the imagination of many readers worldwide. Many overseas readers have flooded IPP Review with comments and inquiries on these articles. Hence IPP Review decided to compile the papers into a book in response to the popular demand.

Part 1 of the book talked about today's Shunde; it has five chapters introducing the district. One should note that in the past 41 years, Shunde has gone through two organisational transformations. First was the change from a county to a county-level city in 1992, the second organisational change was the change from county-level city to an administrative district of Foshan City in 2003. In this book, we used the term county, city and district somewhat interchangeably. The first chapter provides a general introduction to the district; the second chapter introduces its vibrant Lingnan culture; the third chapter talks about the variety of modern and traditional cultural life in Shunde today; the fourth chapter discussed the famous Shunde culinary art and the booming food industry built on the culinary art; the fifth chapter presents some well-known celebrities of Shunde. These chapters tried to present the physical and cultural perspectives of Shunde to the readers.

Part 2 of the book discussed the economic success story of Shunde; we used a lot of historical narratives to show how the district combined its enterprising private sector with the highly capable reform-oriented local government to become a national beacon of reforms in the 1980s and 1990s. The famous visit of Deng Xiaoping to Shunde in February 1992 opened the wave of privatisation of the 1990s which transformed the national economy from an erstwhile state-dominated one to the mixed economy of private ownership complementing state-owned sector, hence the socialist economy with Chinese characteristics.

Chapter 6 talked about the economic phenomenon of Shunde, emphasising the role of government-initiated reforms on the economic transformation from an agricultural backwater to a bustling industrial enclave. It pointed out that manufacturing is the pillar of the economy since the 1980s and the formation of industrial clusters is a natural development arising from the private sector-led industrial sector.

Chapter 7 provided a historical narrative of how Shunde integrated into the global economy. The entrepreneurs of Shunde were the first batch of Chinese businessmen exposed to international trading rules and quality standards. They are quick learners, and also very innovative in bringing out new products after learning and very savvy in building up local brands. They are very focused on their niche operations and quick to go overseas after achieving a certain scale of operations.

Chapter 8 discussed the innovation culture of local private entrepreneurs. We use historical narratives to highlight their early realisation of using innovation as a competitive advantage in gaining market share.

Chapter 9 talked about the history of reforms in Shunde. The district was an acknowledged pioneer in reform since the reform and opening up of the country in 1978. The traditional value of pragmatism, hard work and humility accorded the right cultural elements for trying out new ideas and adjust them to facilitate implementation on the ground. The district remains as the choice location for Guangdong provincial government in trying out new reform measures even as its importance on economic reform has been eclipsed in recent years by Shenzhen.

Chapter 10 discussed the emerging industries of Shunde, highlighting the move toward higher value-added activities like smart manufacturing and robotics, industrial design, modern exhibitions and tourism, and e-commerce.

Chapter 11 touched on the industrial parks and highlighted how the district aims to transform the legacy of old industrial parks into a new modern industrial hub that will facilitate cluster formation, but also encourage the emerging industries through communal facilities provided by the government. The importance of the Sino-German Industrial Services Zone in the drive for smart manufacturing and robotics is also discussed.

Chapter 12 discussed the business environment of the district, highlighting the systematic approach by the district government toward industrial competitiveness.

Chapter 3 talked about the successful companies of Shunde, highlighting the vital role played by the inspirational founders behind these companies' successes.

Part 3 of the book discussed the holistic approach to development adopted by the Shunde government since the 1980s. The district was the first locality in China to experiment on social security as early as 1984. The local government's emphasis on social equity allowed it to push for privatisation in 1992 following Deng Xiaoping's famous 'Southern Tour' (*nanxun*) without any social upheaval or opposition. The emphasis of social reform to go with economic growth and putting livelihood at the centre of any reform minimise social tension and allow reform to proceed sans worry over its sustainability.

Chapter 14 discussed the governance philosophy of Shunde in reform, pointing out that the district government focuses on both hard aspects of urban governance such as building a liveable city and soft governance aspects such as livelihood and transparency.

Chapter 15 traced the history of urbanisation of Shunde. The district's urban population ratio has exceeded 98% and is one of the most urbanised areas in China. Comparing the urban population ratio of less than 20% in 1978, the speed of urbanisation is breakneck even by Chinese standard. An outstanding achievement is the quality of urbanisation has improved significantly in recent years. The district is on the way to become one of the most liveable districts in Guangdong.

Chapter 16 discussed the talent management system of Shunde, noting that the district built up its industries by recruiting and keeping technical talents from other places in China. The openness and pluralistic attitude of the local government and population attracted many 'new Shunde people' to move to the district and contribute to the vibrancy of the manufacturing economy.

Chapter 17 discussed the education system of Shunde, noting that the district's educational setup has a strong vocational orientation. The system tried to match educational outcome with the requirement of the industry, and it has served the district quite well until now. With the move toward higher value-added economic activities, the district is moving upscale in its education outcome.

Part 4 of the book looked into the future of Shunde by exploring the potential role of Shunde in the Guangdong-Hong Kong-Macau Greater Bay Area (GBA). The chapter dissects the strengths and weaknesses of the district as compared to other competing areas in the GBA.

The success story of a dynamic place like Shunde cannot be described adequately in 18 papers. We hope that interested readers would continue to follow the progress of the district after reading this book. There are many valuable lessons one can learn from the development history of the place. We hope that readers can have some take away after reading the book.

I must thank the project manager of the Shunde series of article, Ms Xie Na for her management of the project, Ms Cheong Chean Chian for her excellent editing work, the IPP Review Research Group for writing four chapters on education, culinary culture, celebrities and cultural life. The book will not be complete without these four chapters. I also wish to thank Ms Sylvia Chan for translating most of the chapters from the original Chinese language version to English. The book will not be possible without her work.

Henry Hing Lee Chan PhD

Part 1
Shunde Today

Chapter 1

Shunde: A General Introduction

Shunde is one of the five administrative districts of Foshan city in Guangdong province. It is located in the middle of the Pearl River Delta and is adjacent to Guangzhou, the central city of the Delta. Shunde is also near to Guangzhou South Railway Station, Nansha Port, Baiyun Airport and other important transport hubs in Guangzhou. The district is also adjacent to Zhongshan and Jiangmen. As the newly built longest bridge in the world — the 55-kilometre long Hong Kong-Zhuhai-Macau Bridge is just about one hour's drive from Shunde, the district enjoys easy access to Hong Kong and Macau. Shunde is in the centre of the transport network of the Greater Bay Area.

The land area of Shunde is 806 square kilometres, and it has 205 villages (communities) under four subdistricts and six towns. Ranked by population, the four subdistricts are Daliang, Ronggui, Leliu and Lunjiao, and the six towns namely Xingtan, Beijiao, Lecong, Longjiang, Junan and Chencun. The resident population is 2.61 million, and the population with resident registration (*hukou*) numbered 1.39 million at the end of 2017. There are more than 500,000 Shunde people who are living overseas. As of the end of 2017, 98.58% of the permanent residents in Shunde live in the urban area. Based on the urban area population ratio, Shunde is a highly urbanised district in China.

Figure 1. Vicinity within one hundred kilometres of Shunde

Table 1. Shunde subdistrict/town overview

Subdistrict/Town	Area (km^2)	*Hukou* Population (based on 2017 figures)
Daliang	80.29	252431
Ronggui	80.27	226212
Leliu	90.78	124495
Lunjiao	59.30	94128
Xingtan	121.98	139401
Beijiao	92.11	142514
Lecong	77.85	120668
Longjiang	73.85	109179
Junan	79.45	93946
Chencun	50.70	89697
Total	806.57	1392671

Geography and climate of Shunde

Shunde is located in the central area of the Pearl River Delta, with more than 2.5 kilometres of waterways per square kilometre. The criss-cross river network accounts for 37.4% of the entire area of the district. Most of Shunde's land consists of fertile alluvial plains, endowing the area with one of the most favourable agricultural production conditions in China. Shunde has been one of the wealthiest counties in China since the time of the Song dynasty.

The climate is sub-tropical with a yearly average temperature of 22.3°C. The temperature in winter rarely drops below 10°C, and for more than one-third of the year, it stays above 30°C. Annual humidity ranges from 72% in December to 85% from April to June.

History of Shunde

Shunde's history can be traced back to Qin dynasty (221–206 BC) when the central government set up the Nanhai county in the area. The place remained sparsely populated until the late Song dynasty (960–1279 AD) when northerners massively migrated to Guangdong province to escape from the onslaught of the Mongols. The official name 'Shunde county' was adopted in 1452 AD during the Ming dynasty.

In 1992, Shunde county became a county-level city and was renamed Shunde city. In 2003, Shunde city was absorbed by Foshan — the neighbouring prefecture-level city, and became one of its districts.

As early as the Song dynasty, the place was well-known as the county abounding with fish, fruit, and rice. In the Ming dynasty, the implementation of the integrated mulberry tree and fish pond agronomy model helped the establishment of Shunde's silk industry. Shunde became the famous 'Silk Capital of South China' and the 'Bank of Canton' by the end of the 19th century and the early 20th century. The latter designation reflected the wealth accumulated by Shunde's wealthy merchants in silk and other trades that underpinned the banks at the nearby provincial capital — Canton (Guangzhou).

The economic history of Shunde is more important than its political one. The district has repeatedly played a crucial pioneering role in China's reform and opening up that began in 1978.

Shunde is a microcosm of China's success story

Shunde is a pioneer in the opening up of China in the 1980s. It set up some of the first 'three-plus-one' cooperative trade enterprises of the country as early as the late 1970s. The 'three-plus-one' model means the mainland factory take the three items — materials for processing, materials for assembling, and the product sample — and the 'one' refers to the compensation for the labour provided in the production.

In short, the state-owned or collective enterprise processed imported raw materials, manufactured or assembled products according to the imported samples, and used the products to repay imported equipment and technology loans provided by foreign companies. Shunde established the 'Shunde model' for the development of township enterprises and became the first of the 'Four Tiger Cubs of Guangdong'.

The 'three-plus-one' model became popular in the Chinese coastal area in the late 1980s, with all the participating enterprises exporting their products abroad. By earning the processing fee, they become the primary driving force of the economy. This model played a vital role in promoting China's trade development during the early 20 years of China's reform and opening up. Until now, various forms of processing trade still account for a sizeable part of China's total export trade.

Shunde is also a pioneer in China's property rights reform. In 1992, Shunde was identified by Guangdong provincial government as a comprehensive reform pilot county (city) which took the lead in promoting comprehensive reforms with the reform of the property rights system as the core. Since then, a large number of state-owned enterprises and collective enterprises were privatised. The Shunde experience was replicated in many parts of the country. In 2018, two of the world's Fortune 500 companies came from Shunde: Midea (ranked 323) and Country Garden (ranked 353), and both were the products of privatisation in the early 1990s. The 1992 reforms laid the basis of the Shunde economic model, which is dominated by private enterprises.

In 1999, Shunde was missioned to be 'the pilot city taking the lead in basically realising modernisation'. In 2009, Shunde was identified as a pilot area for the implementation of the 'Scientific Outlook on Development' and took the lead in launching a series of comprehensive reform experiments focusing on administrative system reform, social system reform and grass-roots governance reform. In 2018, Shunde was approved to build the pilot zone for the reform and innovation of high-quality development system in Guangdong province.

The ingenuity of Shunde's populace in charting new paths has contributed to it being chosen as the pilot area whenever the central government starts a new wave of reforms. Since the reform era of 1978, Shunde's people have been taking advantage of its geographic position, the flexible and highly adaptable policy-making government structure, and the ingenuity of its own people. They have transformed Shunde from a traditional agricultural county into a fast-growing industrial district marching towards the new technology-based economy. At the same time, they have shared their development experience with others and have promoted the overall growth of the country.

The culture of Shunde

Shunde has a long and rich cultural heritage. The county produced famous painters such as Li Zichang, Zhao Xianming, and Liang Yuanzhu in Ming dynasty (1368–1644 AD). The renowned painter Li Jian and calligrapher Su Renshan in Qing dynasty were both from Shunde. Among the nine Guangdong top-performing scholars of the imperial court examination from Song to Qing dynasties (960–1911 AD), three are from Shunde.

Shunde is considered one of the cultural hubs of Guangdong. It has 24 items of intangible cultural heritage. It is one of the birthplaces of Cantonese opera. Of the five popular singing styles of the Cantonese opera, three can be traced to Shunde's opera singers. In 2007, Shunde was declared 'The Chinese Folk Art Hometown' in recognition of its contributions to Cantonese folk opera.

The rise of modern textiles relegated the Shunde silk industry to irrelevance in the 20th century. However, the handcrafted gambier Canton gauze (gambier Canton silk) maintains its niche, featuring the unique silk production process of repeatedly dyeing the silk with gambier juice and then covering it with iron-rich native soil, adding an exclusive bactericidal property to the silk. The silk is ideal for buyers who suffer from skin allergies. The handcrafted silk has an annual production of around 200,000 metres and often serves as a souvenir item representing Shunde.

Figure 2. The folk culture of Shunde. Leftmost clockwise: Cantonese opera, production of gambier Canton silk, Shunde gastronomy, martial arts, dragon boats, Qing Hui Garden

The most famous Shunde cultural heritage is undoubtedly its culinary arts. In 2014, UNESCO proclaimed Shunde as a 'City of Gastronomy' under the UNESCO Creative Cities Network, and it was the second Chinese city after Chengdu to receive the coveted award. A famous saying in China goes, 'Eat at Guangzhou, but the cook must be from Shunde' — highlighting the culinary skills of Shunde's chefs. Guangzhou is the provincial capital with the complete assortment of ingredients, highest consumption power, and most significant appreciation for good food. However, it is the culinary skill of Shunde's chefs which transform the ingredients into delicious food. The legend goes that a good Shunde chef can cook a fish in 200 different ways.

Cantonese cuisine is one of the eight major Chinese culinary types, and it emphasises the natural flavours of the ingredients and avoids the use of condiments. The people of Shunde were among the earliest emigrants who went abroad at the end of the 19th century in search of a better life, and they often brought their culinary arts along with them and operated Chinese restaurants anywhere they settled. Many foreigners today take Cantonese food to be representative of Chinese cuisine.

The most famous personality of Shunde is Bruce Lee (1940–1973), the kung-fu superstar who passed away at the young age of 33. His father was

Lee Hoi-Chuen, a famous Cantonese opera singer who hailed from Shunde. Although Bruce Lee was born in the United States and never lived in Shunde, the people of Shunde still consider him to be their folk hero, and they have built a park in his memory.

Dragon boat racing is another famous cultural heritage of Shunde. Every year on the 5th day of the 5th month of the lunar calendar, Shunde's residents will unearth the dragon boats that they buried the previous year and compete in a dragon boat race. The entire village will watch the race and then dine together. After the dragon boat race and the dinner, the people will bury the dragon boats again under the mud of the riverbed in the shallow waters nearby. Shunde is known as the 'Hometown of Chinese Dragon Boats'.

An outstanding architectural relic of Shunde is the Qing Hui Garden, built in 1621 by Huang Shijun (1570–1661 AD), one of the top scholars in the imperial examination. The 3,400 square metre garden is considered a classic Chinese garden with unique Southern Chinese elements. It is considered to be one of the top ten traditional Chinese gardens in the country.

Transportation in Shunde

The Shunde transportation network is one of the most developed in the country. The road density in the district is more than 200 kilometre per 100 square kilometre, which is higher than other cities in the Pearl River Delta. It is also way above the national average of less than 50 kilometre per 100 square kilometre.

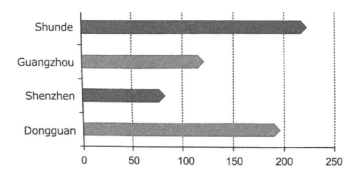

Figure 3. Road density in the cities of the Pearl River Delta (km per 100 square km)

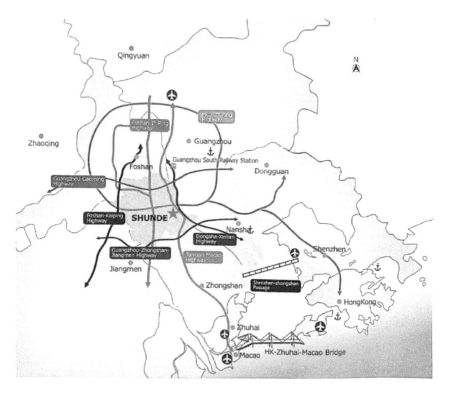

Figure 4. Highway network of Shunde

Shunde has invested substantially in its district road network in recent years. There are seven highways which traverse Shunde, covering all ten subdistricts and towns. Shunde's highway length of 108 kilometre at 13.4 kilometre per 100 square kilometre is three-and-a-half times that of Guangdong's provincial average and is almost ten times the national average. The city road network is now 30:15, that is, 30 minutes to each town, and 15 minutes to the highway entrance from anywhere in Shunde.

Shunde's railway and subway transportation have improved significantly in recent years. The Guangzhou-Zhuhai Intercity Railway was completed in 2012, and there are five stations at Shunde. The second phase of the Guangzhou-Foshan Metro Line 1 connects to Foshan New Town (Lecong Town in Shunde). The Guangzhou-Foshan Ring Line, Foshan Metro Line 2

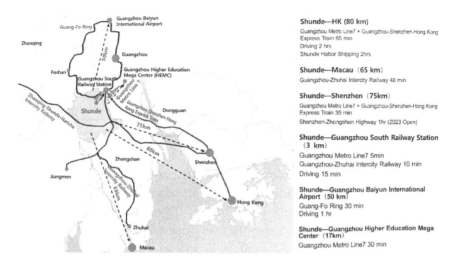

Figure 5. Shunde railway network link with nearby key destinations

and Line 3, and the Guangzhou Metro Line 7 extension are under construction and are expected to be completed by 2022.

Guangzhou Baiyun Airport and the Guangzhou South Railway Station are the regional air and rail hubs of Southern China. Their excellent connections with Shunde makes the district one of the most convenient places to reach in China.

The Shunde Rongqi cargo port has ten berths that can accommodate inland cargo vessels as large as 3,000 tons. The port is the third largest inland water cargo port in Guangdong province and handles 800,000 containers in addition to three million tons of other general cargo annually. Smaller multi-berth inland water ports at Beijiao and Leliu can handle smaller cargo vessel of 2,000 and 1,500 tons respectively. The new Shunde cargo port can berth ships as large as 5,000 tons, but the annual throughput is smaller at 96,000 containers and 1.6 million tons of general cargo in its initial phase. The four cargo ports provide linkages to the principal container ports at Guangzhou, Shenzhen, and Hong Kong.

There is a passenger terminal at Shunde port that provides ten trips to Hong Kong daily. The connectivity of Shunde by air, land, and sea is excellent for both cargo and passengers.

The Shunde economy: Industry at its core

Shunde is a substantial manufacturing base in the Pearl River Delta. In 2017, the primary, secondary and tertiary industries of Shunde was 1.5%: 56.3%: and 42.3%. Shunde's industry is characterised by industrial clusters, local brands, private enterprises and a high proportion of local components in their products.

In 2017, Shunde had eight pillar industries, including home appliances, machinery and equipment, furniture manufacturing, fine chemicals, information and communications technology, textiles and garments, printing and packaging, and medicine and health care. The industrial output value of the eight pillar industries accounted for 77.8% of the industrial output value of enterprises above a certain designated size. In recent years, Shunde has successfully developed three major industries, that is, jewellery, auto parts and lighting. Thanks to the considerable manufacturing industry in Shunde, the e-commerce trade has also risen rapidly.

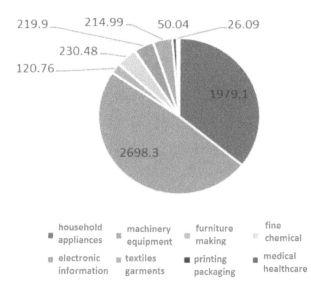

Figure 6. The production value of eight pillar industries of Shunde

Shunde's industrial clustering

Industrial clustering is an outstanding feature among the townships of Shunde. Eight out of the ten subdistricts and towns have their traditional signature industries. The district ranked for seven consecutive years (2012–2018) as the top district in the 'Top 100 Districts of Comprehensive Competitiveness'.

The home appliances industry is an apt illustration of industrial clustering. The home appliances cluster located at Beijiao and Ronggui has more than 3,200 companies in different parts of the production chain. A vast majority of the companies in the cluster are privately owned, and the presence of both large, medium and small players in the industrial production chain allows for specialisation and complementation. The industry associations play a crucial role in technology sharing, and demonstrate Shunde's great entrepreneurial spirit.

Shunde has developed numerous home appliances brands. By the end of 2017, Shunde had nine nationally famous brands — Midea, Hisense Kelon, Macro, Galanz, Ronshen, Vanward, Canbo, DonLim and Bear, which account for almost one-third of all nationally famous home appliances brands. It also has 31 well-known Guangdong provincial brands. There are also 57 popular Guangdong provincial products, such as Midea refrigerators, Kelon air-conditioners, Galanz microwave ovens, Macro gas heaters and water heaters, and Vanward gas heaters.

Figure 7. Industrial clusters in Shunde townships

A similar industrial situation can be found in the other pillar industries. The robust industrial clustering which maximises local component inputs and holds down costs, the development of local brands which produce quality products, the private sector domination of businesses and the entrepreneurship of Shunde's businessmen, are intangibles behind the success of Shunde as the bastion of local privately-owned manufacturers in China. By the end of 2017, there were 74 private businesses with annual sales of more than one billion yuan in Shunde. These are called the 'hidden champions' in their respective fields. The private sector accounted for more than 77% of industrial production in 2017.

Shunde runs a large trade surplus as compared to other cities in the Pearl River Delta. The district exported 138.31 billion yuan and imported 38.13 billion yuan in 2017. This figure can be contrasted to Dongguan city's export value of 702.74 billion yuan and import value of 523.7 billion yuan and the corresponding values of 1,653.36 billion yuan and 1,147.79 billion yuan for Shenzhen. The comparison illustrates the success of the locally centric industrial model of Shunde in keeping its earnings at home.

At the moment, Shunde is working on industrial upgrading in its pillar industries through projects implementing Technology Shunde. The home appliances and other pillar industries are facing the pressures of fast-changing technology and rising labour costs. Hence there is a call for smart manufacturing to keep costs down and quality up. One of the critical industrial transformation goals is to implement intelligent manufacturing systems in the pillar industries. The government is setting up a robotation (robots plus automation) industrial park with Midea and KUKA to draw multinational and private companies to the location. The emergence in recent years of robotics companies in Shunde attests to the progress in this area.

The Shunde government is implementing the strategy of 'One City, Three Areas', focusing on building the Shunde New Downtown. The northern part will focus on industrial services and innovation, and the key development platform is the Sino-German Industrial Services Area. The eastern district will be an intelligent zone led by scientific research groups and financial departments, with a focus on the Southern Wisdom Valley. The southwest area will develop environmental protection technology and intelligent manufacturing technology to meet the needs of industrial upgrading and innovation. The key platform is the Shunde High-Tech Zone.

Figure 8.   'One City, Three Areas' development plan

Shunde is a manufacturing hub in the Greater Bay Area of Guangdong, Hong Kong and Macau. In the future of the Greater Bay Area, Shunde will play an important role in the smart manufacturing industry and other manufacturing industries in which Shunde has production advantages.

Conclusion

Shunde's story is a microcosm of China's reform and development. The Shunde model counts among other successful regional economic models, including those of Shenzhen, Kunshan, Dongguan, and others. A closer look at the Shunde model will reveal the challenges and possible solutions to the continuing reforms that China must undertake now to avoid the 'middle-income trap' and the difficulties that will arise from its economic transformation.

Chapter 2

Shunde's Lingnan Culture

Shunde is located in the central part of the Pearl River Delta Plain. Apart from mountains in the north, southeast and south, most of its terrain is flat, and the river network occupies more than one-third of the whole area. This geographical condition has created a favourable environment for the development of maritime traffic and commercial trade. After the ban on sea trade during the Ming and Qing dynasties was lifted, Shunde became China's gateway to the outside world and was also one of the important hinterlands of the Pearl River Delta in Guangzhou. Shunde's interaction with foreign countries is way ahead of other coastal areas.

Lingnan is the generic name for the area south of the Five Ridges in southern China. The Five Ridges are Yuechengling, Dupangling, Mengzhuling, Qitianling and Dayuling and are located in the eastern part of Guangxi to the eastern part of Guangdong and between Hunan and Jiangxi provinces. Since the Han dynasty, Lingnan has been occupied by three major dialect groups: Guangfu, Kejia and Minnan. The Lingnan area, far from the Chinese mainland, surrounded by the Five Ridges and facing the sea, has formed a unique Lingnan culture.

Long-term foreign trade and contacts have made the Lingnan culture a melting pot of cultural exchanges between China and foreign countries, and it has made a tremendous impact on modern China. Since the reform and opening up, the Lingnan culture has played a positive role in promoting China's economic and social development with its unique characteristics of pluralism, pragmatism, openness, compatibility and innovation. It is one of the most distinctive and dynamic regional cultures in China.

The region, which is located near the border, has abundant agricultural resources and its foreign trade started earlier than others. In a thriving market economy, Shunde refuses empty talk and focuses on a pragmatic Lingnan culture.

This article focuses on three key parts of Shunde's culture: dragon boat racing, cuisine and ancestral halls, and analyses how they provide cultural and spiritual support for Shunde's success in reform and opening up.

Dragon boat racing is a valuable culture of Shunde

Shunde has an expansive river network, where the river is at the doorstep and getting around by water transport is very convenient. In the integrated mulberry tree and fish pond agronomy model, people travelled by boat to most places. When they came across each other's boats, they would compete to see who could row their boat faster. This is one of the origins of dragon boat racing in Shunde.

Dragon boat racing has a history of two thousand years in Shunde. According to research, the dragon boat race was a traditional custom of the ancient Yue people. The Dragon Boat Festival was a festival in which the Yue people worshipped to totems for peaceful lives. According to literature, Shunde has always had a custom of dragon boat racing throughout the different eras. In the past, while having an agricultural respite in the summers and autumns, the townships would hold dragon boat races of various sizes. Today, dragon boat racing in the Pearl River Delta is a popular sport, and Shunde has the most famous races in the Pearl River Delta. There are dragon boat teams in almost every village in Shunde.

Shunde's Dragon Boat Festival has many rituals. Before the game, the 'Painting the Dragon's Eyes' ceremony will be held. Every year on the third day of the fifth month of the lunar calendar, the Longyan Village in Leliu, Shunde will hold a 'Painting the Dragon's Eyes' ceremony. More than 120 dragon boats in the Pearl River Delta region will gather in the village's Taiwei Temple to have their 'eyes' painted to awaken the 'sleeping dragon'. This ceremony in Longyan Village has a history of more than 600 years and has been included in the provincial intangible cultural heritage. It has become the symbol of the dragon boat racing culture in Shunde.

Shunde's annual dragon boat racing activities are held from May 1 International Labour Day to November, with the fourth to the sixth day of the fifth month of the lunar calendar being the busiest. Every year, there are more than a million people attending the festival. Dragon boat racing is the oldest sports programme in Shunde and has won Shunde the reputation of 'the hometown of dragon boat' in 2005.

In Shunde, the magical and ever-lasting dragon boat racing culture is deeply ingrained and widely promulgated. It has become a ubiquitous cultural legacy and regional soft power. It also exemplifies the most outstanding qualities of the Shunde people:

(1) Unity and teamwork. Since the reform and opening up, Shunde people have focused on the overall situation of economic construction, and have taken the lead in establishing industrial counties and developing township and village enterprises. They are concentrating on developing the economy and leading the country. Today, more than 2.7 million Shunde people, half of which are registered population and half of which are resident population, are united with the same goal, that is, to build Shunde into a beautiful home.

(2) Pioneering and fearless. Whether it is enterprise development, science and technology education, medical care, social security, urban construction or cultural development, Shunde is advancing in all directions and striving to be the best. It has successfully transformed from a traditional agricultural county to a modern industrial city; it has been leading the way, and its comprehensive strength has been at the forefront of China's counties for many years. Midea and Country Garden grew from small enterprises to large corporations and entered the ranks of the Global Fortune 500. Entrepreneurs such as He Xiangjian, Yang Guoqiang and Liang Qingde have become famous businessmen through their efforts and struggles.

(3) Humble and unrelenting. In the process of reform and opening up and innovation and development, the Shunde people are not sitting on their laurels, and they are not afraid of uncertainty. In industry, they keep making innovations; in system reform, they keep persevering; in urban construction, they keep renewing and altering; in cultural development, they keep preserving and updating. Shunde people always maintain a

strong fighting spirit, have the confidence to win, and persist in struggle. Shunde has been bravely leading the way, continually developing and tapping potential.

(4) Hardworking and improving. Shunde people are low-key and pragmatic; they do not dream or fantasise and do not like empty talk. They believe that actions speak louder than words and with actual efforts, the fruits of labour can be harvested. Today, Shunde is once again calling its people not to seek comforts and believe that victory comes from real struggle.

(5) Fair and respectful. Regardless of the competition or the market, Shunde people always respect the rules, fully recognise the achievements and strengths of others, and learn with humility. They strive to win competitions on the strengths of their products and services in order to establish their social and economic status. Shunde people adopt an open-minded attitude to learn from the strengths of others, so as to stand out from the competition.

Many people attribute Shunde's industrial success to the above-mentioned dragon boat racing spirit: unity in goal, striving forward, challenging oneself, never gives up and being fair in competition. Many regions in China have attempted to follow Shunde's experience in industrial development, but there are only a handful of successes. The influence of regional culture on economic growth can be seen through the experience of Shunde.

Shunde's cuisine reflects its precious craftsmanship

The most famous facet of Shunde's culture is undoubtedly its culinary art. In 2014, Shunde officially became a member of the UNESCO Creative City Network — the City of Gastronomy, the second Chinese city to receive this award after Chengdu. (If you want to know more about Shunde's cuisine, please refer to the article 'Shunde's Culinary Culture and Food Industry')

The style of Shunde cuisine originated from the Qin and Han dynasties. After thousands of years of inheritance and improvement, it has become the foundation of Shunde's culture with its long history and diverse cooking materials and methods. In general, Shunde's families start to teach their children, no matter boy or girl, simple cooking from a young age. The whole family cooking together is a part of family life, and many families have their special recipes. The most popular family recipes are stir-fries.

Every year, the ten towns and streets of Shunde will hold a family special recipe cooking competition, attracting thousands of people every time. From the seniors of ages 70 to 80 to teenagers, Shunde's vibrant food culture comes from countless ordinary people. During the festival, the whole village or whole clan will gather around to eat. All of Shunde's people are chefs in their own right. From the top professional chefs to the lowest level of ordinary citizens, they are all culinary masters, forming a multi-level food community with a solid foundation and endless creativity.

The most important aspect behind Shunde's food culture is the pursuit of the ultimate 'artisan spirit'. Culinary expertise needs to be accumulated over a long time, which is a reflection of the development and personal cultivation of the 'artisan spirit'.

In the late 1980s, Shunde imported low-end electric fans, air conditioners and other products from Hong Kong, Taiwan, and Japan, and gradually established the production and export capabilities of its own electric fans and air conditioners. From low-end to high-end, the process from imitation to independent research and development is also Shunde's embodiment of the 'artisan spirits'.

Many entrepreneurs in Shunde are willing to go in-depth in one professional field, which is also the embodiment of this spirit. In the home appliances manufacturing industry, which is the pride of Shunde, many companies produce a single product with an output value of 500 million to a billion yuan, except for big corporations such as Midea. This level of professionalism is rare in other places in China. (For details, see the article 'Shunde's Innovations'.)

Ancestral halls represent the cohesiveness and localness of Shunde's culture

Shunde is famous for its many sprawling ancestral halls. In the vast rural areas of Shunde, villages are formed by clans of relatives living together, and almost all villages have their ancestral halls. The ancestral hall has become a means of managing the clan, strengthening clan power, improving one's social status and enhancing business reputations.

Shunde's ancestral halls were first built in the Song and Yuan dynasties and flourished in the Ming and Qing dynasties. In the middle and late Qing dynasty, ancestral halls of all sizes were found all over the urban and rural areas, and the total number could have exceeded ten thousand. Today, there are about 500 preserved ancestral halls in Shunde, including more than 200 protected cultural relics at the provincial, municipal and district levels. In recent years, with the support of local governments and villages, Shunde's ancestral halls are restored and protected, not only for inheriting the traditional culture, but also for turning them into new public cultural spaces, for the purposes of cultural relics protection, regional culture collection and display, tourism, education and entertainment.

It is worth mentioning that Shunde produced the largest number of top scholars in the imperial examinations from Guangdong province. In just over 500 years, there had been three top scholars, more than 300 *'jinshi'* and more than 2,000 *'juren'* from Shunde (both *'jinshi'* and *'juren'* refers to successful candidates in the imperial court examinations and provincial level examinations in the past). Shunde not only achieved a strong economic foundation but also placed great importance on education. Many ancestral halls ran private schools either directly or indirectly. The rental from the ancestral halls' fields, after deducting for sacrificial ceremonies, was used for the studies expenses of the males in the family, fees for students attending the examinations, and the costs for the trip to the capital Beijing for the examinations. The subsidy had played a positive role in enhancing the overall cultural standards of the Shunde people and producing top scholars in the imperial examinations.

In the 21st century, Shunde, after making remarkable achievements in economic development, is attaching great importance to cultural undertakings. The government and the people realise that the ancestral hall carries historical and cultural connotations, which are the crystallisation of the traditional folk culture of Shunde and the symbol of the cohesiveness and affinity of the clans. Therefore, all of society has begun to invest in the repair of Shunde's ancestral halls.

Today, some of the ancestral halls have begun to play other roles, such as the village history exhibition hall, the farmer's book house, the art club, the special exhibition room, the elderly activity centre and the fitness and entertainment area. They have become a place where the villagers go to for entertainment, fitness, learning knowledge and chatting. The ancestral hall has become a central point for rolling out social services in rural areas.

Clan cohesion, affinity and localness, as represented by the ancestral hall culture, are considered to be the characteristics of Shunde's private entrepreneurs. In the early days of reform and opening up, successful entrepreneurs from Hong Kong and Macau returned to Shunde to build schools and hospitals. Today, successful entrepreneurs from Shunde build charities and actively train corporate talents. All of these reflect the ancestral hall culture of Shunde.

Other intangible cultural heritages

Shunde is an important area of Lingnan culture, and there are many intangible cultural heritages here. An intangible cultural heritage at the national level, the handcrafted gambier Canton silk gets its name — *Xiangyunsha* — from its lightweight fabric making 'shasha' sounds when worn by a person. The *Xiangyunsha* has a unique silk production process of repeatedly dyeing the silk with gambier juice, and then covering it with iron-rich native soil which adds an exclusive bactericidal property to the silk, imbibing it with the function of preventing skin allergies. The Shunde district government presents *Xiangyunsha* as a gift to important foreign guests as a speciality of Shunde.

Readers who are interested in other intangible cultural heritages can access online information about the following items to gain a deeper understanding of Shunde's culture:

There are 4 national intangible cultural heritages, including *Xiangyunsha*, dragon boat folksongs, dragon dance, and 8-sounds drums.

There are 7 provincial intangible cultural heritages, including Chencun flower show, Guangdong embroidery, *Guanyin* worship, *Zhenbutang* astronomical calendar, Cantonese opera, *Guandi Houwang* parade, and painting the dragon's eyes custom.

There are 17 intangible cultural heritages at the city and district level, including dragon boat racing, water village farming customs, spring festival customs, Wing Chun martial arts, Cantonese opera, dragon mother's birthday, water village folksong, Shunde cooking skills, porridge water making skills, Daliang fish lamp making skills, double-layer milk custard making skills, Lunjiao rice cake making skills, Chencun noodle-making skills, Hung Ga martial arts, dragon boat carving skills, Nansha wedding customs, wedding cake making skills.

Conclusion

The spirit of Shunde's Lingnan culture provided an intangible spiritual environment for Shunde in the reform era and provided the invisible drive to promote the take-off of the economy. Today, the Shunde economy needs further transformation and upgrading, and the same Shunde spirit will likely push the city forward.

Chapter 3

Shunde's Cultural Life

At a time when tradition and modernity are at the crossroads, Shunde has managed to preserve its traditional culture yet embrace new ones. On the one hand, Shunde promotes local arts and customs, and on the other, it opens its doors to different cultures by facilitating exchange. During the year, a wide array of activities is available to the public, such as the 'Dragon Boat Festival', 'Fifty-kilometre Walk', 'Water Canal Festival', 'Chinese Literature Week' and 'Sino-French Cultural Exchange'. Whether you are a first-time visitor or a foreigner living in Shunde, you will be able to experience the district's inclusive and dynamic cultural environment and fall in love with the place.

This article attempts to highlight the diverse ways in which Shunde fuses tradition and modernity by introducing some of the locals' favourite festivities.

Fusing tradition and modernity

The coexistence of tradition and modernity in Shunde is a norm in contemporary Chinese society. On the traditional front, modern Shunde folks still lead a life that is steeped in tradition: listening and watching Cantonese opera, visiting ancestral temples and monuments, appreciating relics, enjoying local cuisine, cheering during dragon boat competition and so on. While immersing themselves in traditional activities, Shunde locals also actively disseminate these cultural heritages to the international community. Every year Shunde hosts a vast number of domestic and foreign tourists who are interested in experiencing Shunde's local culture and cuisine. On the modernity front, Shunde people also enjoy new lifestyle alternatives: going to the opera house to watch plays and concerts, participating in nationwide fitness programmes and youth sports activities and so on.

The ability to enjoy traditional cultural activities and embrace the new western way of life is a result of the economic prosperity in Shunde. The interaction between old and new generates a beneficial circular flow between the cultural sector and the economy; while people have the financial means to spend more time on leisure and engage in cultural activities, the flourishing cultural life boosts the cultural service sector of the economy.

Grassroots cultural carnival

Shunde's rich cultural heritage is not only a representation of its history and legacy, but also the spiritual backbone behind the district's continuous progress. In September 2018, the Shunde government collaborated with the media and launched the 'Shunde District Ancient Village Cultural Upgrade Programme'. Organised at the grassroots level, the 2018 cultural carnival hosted a series of activities that lasted for three months and showcased intangible cultural heritage. Locals and tourists had the chance to see the elegant traditional Dragon Dances, hear the unique and catchy 'Dragon Boat Song' which is widely sung in the Pearl River Delta, and visit the exquisite Gambiered Guangdong Gauze exhibition which details the complicated silk yarn making process.

The Wing Chun Kungfu exhibition is popular among Chinese martial arts enthusiasts. Wing Chun is an important school of traditional Southern kungfu. It consists of 12 boxing techniques and six stick play techniques. Wing Chun strengthens both the body and character and remains a popular exercise.

There are many other activities the public can enjoy. They can listen to the band of gongs and drums and enjoy the ceremony of painting the

Table 1. A partial list of cultural programmes in Shunde

Programme type	Programme name (Main theme)	Programme description
Traditional	*Guanyin Budhisattva's* Vault Opening Festival	On January 26 of the lunar calendar, a festival will be held at Bailin Park, Ronggui to pray for the *Guanyin Budhisattva* to open the vault so that believers can pray for wealth. The folk tradition is more than a thousand years old and is popular in the Pearl River Delta.
Traditional	Ceremony of Painting the Dragon's Eye	On May 3 of the lunar calendar, the eye-painting ceremony for the dragon boat will be held at Leliu Longyan Village. Photography and art exhibitions, as well as food festivals, are also held to celebrate the annual dragon boat race.
Traditional	Longtan Water Canal Cultural Festival	On May 8 of the lunar calendar, people will assemble at the Longtan sea goddess temple to pray and celebrate through activities like dragon boat parade.
Traditional	*Guandi Houwang* Parade	Held on September 4 of the lunar calendar at Junan town, the parade has a history of over 160 years. People from 13 villages will parade around the town to pray for good fortune and safety.
Traditional	Shunde Village Banquet	Different villages will hold village-wide banquets during different times of the year to celebrate festivities, for instance, the Shunde Lantern And Wine Festival (lunar January 6-15), Dragon Boat Festival (May), Shunde Cabbage Festival (lunar January 25) and Elders Festival (during Chung Yeung Festival).
Cultural heritage	Cantonese Opera Series	During different times of the year, Shunde holds numerous Cantonese opera shows and concerts at schools, parks, opera houses and other venues.
Cultural heritage	Shunde Water Canal Festival	As part of the national day celebration, the festival is a series of activities celebrating food and dragon boat and includes painting, calligraphy and photo exhibitions.
Cultural heritage	Campus Cultural Talk And Heritage Exhibition	A collaboration between the district museum and higher education institutions to introduce Shunde's history to schools; it includes talks and photo exhibitions regarding famous people, food and tradition.
Cultural heritage	Shunde Interactive And Education Workshop	Held during weekends and holidays at the Shunde district museum, a series of interactive and experiential workshops is conducted for the public to learn Shunde's culture through hands-on activities, such as making Chinese lanterns and dragon boats.

(Continued)

Table 1. (*Continued*)

Programme type	Programme name (Main theme)	Programme description
Traditional and modern culture	Shunde Grassroots Cultural Festival	Aiming to serve the public at the grassroots level, the district sponsors a series of township-based cultural activities throughout the year. For instance, from April 29 to 16 December 2018, 38 dragon boat-based activities were held during the Dragon Boat Festival.
Traditional and modern culture	'Feng Qi Cang Lan' Shunde Light Exhibition	A large-scale, twenty-minute laser light display highlighting Shunde's people, culture, history and landscape. For more information, refer to 'Feng Qi Cang Lan' Shunde Light Exhibition description below.
Modern culture	Chinese Literature Festival	Literature prize set up by the Southern City Daily. It is one of the most prestigious and pure literary awards in China. For more information, refer to 'Literature in Shunde' description below.
Modern culture	Weekend Arts And Culture Festival	A weekend filled with fun and games where different cultural activities sponsored by the local government are held. Activities include dance competitions, art performances and a children's playground.
Modern culture	Shunde Citizen Reading Activity and Youth Summer Reading Camp	Every April, reading activities will be organised by the Shunde district library. The period coincides with World Reading Day on April 23. During the summer holiday (July to August), a youth reading camp will also be organised for migrant children and low-income family children.
Modern culture	Jewellery Tourism Cultural Festival	The festival is held annually in December at Lunjiao street. It showcases jewel design and tourism.
Modern culture	Shunde Wind City Musical Festival And Sino-European Carnival	Shunde's Wind City Music Festival is held at Shunfengshan Park and other art venues. It includes large-scale events like the Sino-French Summer Solstice Music Festival and Guangdong Province Guitar Festival. The Sino-European carnival is held every October to November at Lecong town. It comprises three main activities: beer and culinary festival, dragon boat competition and international Wushu competition.
Modern culture	Chencun mid-summer music festival, Dream Show	The music competition is held every year from July to October.

dragon's eye on the dragon boat (which is said to 'awaken' the dragon), go to the flower festival in Chencun, admire intricate and elegant embroidery, and experience the *Guangyin Budhisattva*'s vault opening festival. Listening to the rich and harmonious Cantonese opera show is also an interesting experience.

Dragon boat race

'One, paint the dragon eye and pray for good weather and the safety of the people; two, paint the forehead and pray to the heavens and for good fortune…' is the melody for the painting of the dragon's eye festival. Following the traditional ceremony of painting the dragon's eye on November 16, 2018, the 13th Asian Dragon Boat Championships commenced at Shunde's Gui Pan Lake.

Shunde is the hometown of Chinese dragon boat. It is one of the favourite activities enjoyed by locals. Under the district's influential dragon boat culture, the Shunde team has won many international awards.

Many of Shunde's customs are related to dragon boat, for instance, painting the dragon eye, singing the dragon boat song, celebrating the dragon mother's birthday and so on. The annual Dragon Boat Festival is one

Figure 1. Dragon boat race

of the most popular cultural events in the region. Combining dragon boat racing and pageant, parade, folklore performance and other activities, the festival attracts more than 1 million spectators annually.

The passion for dragon boat is deeply rooted and widely spread. The sport encourages generations of Shunde people to strive for the best in their life. To know more about Shunde's dragon boat culture, see the article 'Shunde's Lingnan Culture'.

Culinary art in Shunde

Food plays an irreplaceable role in the hearts of Shunde people; ubiquitous restaurants, home-cook restaurants and snack bars lining up the streets is proof of their love of food. In 2018, the Shunde Home Cooking

Figure 2. Award-winning entries from the Shunde Home Cooking competition

Competition which attracted many culinary enthusiasts had already been held 13 times.

Food brings people together. During the festive season, Shunde people like to gather over a good meal and forge deep relationships. Village banquets are held for this reason. The size of each banquet varies from a few to over a hundred tables, and most of the dishes served are simple and home-cooked. The 'Lettuce Festival' held at Liandu Village in Leliu Town is usually the largest banquet of the year. Its origin can be traced to the late-1500s during the Ming dynasty. On the night of every January 25 (lunar calendar), Liandu Village hosts thousands of tables for the banquet. Its record is 2,198 tables and close to 20,000 patrons from Hong Kong, Macau and other neighbouring cities. In recent years, many tour groups have also joined the event. In Cantonese dialect, lettuce is pronounced similarly as the desire to have a year of blessing for wealth and health.

Shunde people are very creative when it comes to culinary arts. For instance, the Chencun Food and Flower Cultural Festival takes advantage of both the floral and cooking skill of the locals, and patrons visiting the festival are treated to a feast of both. Since 2013, the festival has been held

Figure 3. Lettuce Festival

annually. The sixth event in 2018 continued to focus on the village's unique flower and food offerings, with a particular focus on activities like flower banquets and culinary competitions. For more information regarding food culture and industrial development in Shunde, see the article 'Shunde's Culinary Culture and Food Industry'.

'Feng Qi Cang Lan' Shunde Light Exhibition

On the eve of every Chinese New Year, Shunde locals can enjoy a light exhibition boasting the city's culture – its past, present and future – as well as its road to modernisation. The light show is named 'Feng Qi Cang Lan' for two reasons. Firstly, Shunde is known as Phoenix City ('Feng Cheng'); 'Feng Qi' indicates that the phoenix lifts off and that Shunde is revitalised. Secondly, 'Cang Lan' refers to Shunde's geographical position along the South China Sea as well as Shunde's glorious journey since the country's reform and opening up in 1978. The light exhibition has a prologue titled 'My Homeland' and four chapters: 'Strive to be the First', 'The Outstanding People', 'The Charming Place' and 'Pioneering spirit'. The story highlights the essence of the city's past since the economic reform and the daring attitude that led to Shunde's success.

Figure 4. A snippet of the 'Feng Qi Cang Lan' light exhibition

The Shunde Dream Show

The Chencun Shunde Dream Show has been gaining popularity since its inception in 2011. The modern songfest competition provides Shunde residents with a platform to showcase their talent on stage. The winner emerges after several elimination rounds. The show is an important aspect to promote Shunde's lovely countryside and is one of the activities in which the Shunde district government spent six years carefully crafting. In 2018, the show was nominated as a vital supporting programme which promotes Shunde grassroots culture, affirming its contribution towards rural revitalisation.

Literature in Shunde

The Chinese Literature Festival, initiated by Southern City Daily in 2003, has been held in Shunde for 13 consecutive seasons. Upholding the tenets of creativity, independence and freedom of expression in literature, the festival is non-government in nature. The festival is known to be one of the most influential and credible Chinese literature festivals for individual writers in the country. The list of award winners includes Nobel Laureate Mo Yan, Shi Tie-sheng, Han Shao-gong, Jia Ping-wa and many more.

On top of the usual awards ceremony during the festival, the Shunde district government also promote a series of events to encourage the local Lingnan culture. Examples include the Shunde map-reading activity, Shunde Primary School poetry competition, literary week painting and calligraphy exhibition. The events give the public an opportunity to appreciate famous artworks. While promoting Chinese literature to the international community, particular focus is also given to promote Shunde's culture.

Charity in Shunde

Shunde locals are modest and charitable. Those who have achieved success never forget about their roots and actively contribute back to the Shunde society. For instance, He Xiangjian, founder of Midea Group, donated 100 million shares and 2 billion yuan to a Guangdong charity foundation to support social causes like poverty alleviation, education, medical and elderly care in Foshan and the country. Yang Guoqiang, founder of Country Garden, built many schools to provide free education. Likewise, Shunde

Huaqiao Middle School, Shunde Sports Centre and Shunde Vocation School were all funded by outstanding Shunde natives who reside in Hong Kong and Macau.

Migrants are attracted to a city which offers excellent career opportunity, a productive cultural life and a suitable environment for settling down. Shunde has done a excellent job in fostering a hospitable environment; many of its charity work are designed for the underprivileged. During the 2018 Shunde Charity Month, the first 'Charity Organisations Management Standard' was promulgated by the Guangdong provincial government, and its rules set the benchmark for a more regulated and higher-quality charity sector. The new standard is expected to bring more benefits to a broader range of vulnerable groups. Additionally, the new 'Charity+' series created by the Shunde Charity Organisation Alliance was also officially launched during the same month. It combines charity with other elements of Shunde's unique culture and includes projects like 'Charity + Internet', 'Charity + Consumption', 'Charity + Tourism', 'Charity + Culture'. The series not only promotes Shunde's cultural industry but also brings new possibilities and resources for the charity sector.

Experiencing international cultural fusion in Shunde

Shunde blends its diverse modern culture to its centuries-old indigenous culture. Modern science and technology are being integrated into the daily life of locals; at the same time, cultural pride encourages them to spread, promote and interact with other cultures. During this process, the quality of cultural exchange activities has improved and taken root in Shunde. A variety of international activities highlighting Shunde's history and culture were held.

The Sino-French Summer Solstice Music Festival was held in Daliang in June 2018. The aim of the festival is to celebrate Chinese and French culture and is the seventh instalment jointly organised by the Shunde local government office and the French Consulate General in Guangzhou. The theme for the 2018 festival was 'Melody Never Ends', and the focus was on exhibitions and interactive activities relating to Chinese and French music, arts, cuisine and life. Through band performances, creative workshops, consumer interactive experiences and other multifaceted activities, the public experienced the unique charm of Chinese and French cultures.

Figure 5. The Sino-French Summer Solstice Music Festival

In 2016, the Sino-European Cultural Carnival was successfully held as part of the second China (Guangdong) International 'Internet+' exhibition. Through different exhibition booths, the public was able to learn about European, Chinese Lingnan, Wushu, food and other cultures. There were a wide variety of offerings: delicacies from the gourmet section, cultural experiences from the Sino-European and games sections, and even clown shows and live bands that showcase the different cultures. There was also the Wing Chun Invitationals preliminary competition and Chinese Lingnan folk culture exhibition. Participants were genuinely spoilt for choice from the plethora of Chinese and Western cultural activities. The cultural carnival is an opportunity to showcase the development of culture, business and ecology sectors in Northern Shunde. It is also an important long-term strategy to promote regional culture, which is continually being reinvented, developed and spread.

Reconnecting with Shunde's roots

Shunde people are deeply sentimental towards their hometown. Both overseas Shunde people and Shunde residents in other places in China and their

Figure 6. The 11th reunion by the Shunde Worldwide Friendship Association

descendants get together through annual reunions. Since the inaugural grand reunion in 1998, Shunde has successfully held many more gatherings around the world. In May 2018, the 11th Shunde Worldwide Friendship Association reunion was held in Vancouver, Canada. More than 900 people from 50 organisations and 13 countries participated in the reunion. During the two days, overseas Shunde people gathered together to talk about Shunde's development, reminisce their past, enjoy Shunde cuisine and traditional cultural performances and promote communication, which alleviated their homesickness.

Conclusion

Traditional culture serves as an anchor for Shunde people; it is passed from generation to generation and is very much alive today. Unique Shunde values have been ingrained in people's daily lives, and Shunde's open and inclusive way of living and respect for other cultures are attractive to both locals and migrants. The vibrant cultural life has also deepened the Shunde spirit. Traditional and modern culture, food, technology and other elements are important elements which make up today's Shunde.

Economic success has brought a sense of pride and confidence to the Shunde people and deepened their faith over their society. The creative and indomitable entrepreneurial spirit of Shunde people also promotes innovation and development of its cultural life. Shunde people remain humble and steadfast in the face of their achievements and continuously push for more international culture exchange. The Shunde people do not simply bask in their glory but continue to strive for the betterment of Shunde's cultural infrastructure and inject vitality to the economy.

Chapter 4
Shunde's Culinary Culture and Food Industry

As one of the eight major cuisines in China, Cantonese cuisine is famous both at home and abroad for its unique and skilful cooking techniques, fresh seasonal local produce and rich tastes. Shunde is the hinterland of Chinese cuisine and the birthplace of Cantonese cuisine. The warm and humid climate, the flat and open land, the stable and prosperous life and the hardworking local people are the necessary conditions for the development of Shunde's cooking skills and food culture. For Shunde people, food is not only for survival but also for them to go to varied places to create businesses and enterprises. It is a reflection of the spirit of the Shunde people who are truthful, pragmatic and innovative.

Shunde, while holding on to the essence of its traditional food culture, is at the same time using new media and new platforms to promote its food culture. By integrating educational research, brand building and international cooperation, the Shunde district government is creating a unique food culture and industry. Pairing culture and economy in a steady manner can bring about the development of the region. It can also showcase a unique and beautiful Shunde.

The history and style of Shunde food culture

Shunde cuisine is known for having rich ingredients and creative cooking methods. 'Five flavours, six arts, fresh drinks, good food and natural ingredients' is the most accurate summary of the characteristics of Shunde food culture. In olden times, people from the Central Plains migrated to Guangdong province and blended the Central Plains diet with Guangdong's agricultural and fishery resources according to local conditions. This fusion is the origin of Shunde's food culture.

If the natural environment is the soil for the growth of Shunde's food culture, then the skills and craftsmanship are the foundations of the development of its food culture. The integrated mulberry tree and fish pond agronomy model provided the local people with sufficient fish and livestock products and plentiful fruits and vegetables. The developed agricultural economy allowed the well-to-do Shunde people to delve into food and cooking in their leisure time. With their flexible mind and willingness to experiment, Shunde people's love for food and cooking was gradually formed. Shunde is one of four chefs' hometowns in China and enjoys the reputation of 'eat in Guangzhou, but the cook must be from Fengcheng (Shunde)'. As early as the end of the eighteenth century, Shunde chefs began to bring their cooking skills overseas and were unanimously recognised for their proficiencies. They also brought Cantonese cuisine out of the country and made it famous both at home and abroad.

Shunde dishes emphasise natural flavours and exquisiteness, a reflection of the pragmatic and ever-improving Shunde people. Shunde dishes showcase the most natural and most pristine taste of the ingredients. The cooking not only require fresh ingredients, but also precise skills and accurate grasp of the heat and time. Shunde cuisine is also known for its fascinating variations. The freshest seasonal ingredients are selected and cooked by a skilful combination of 24 traditional cooking methods. The chefs' flair can not only retain the natural taste of the ingredients but can also conjure up diverse tastes in distinctive presentations at different times of the year.

Chinese cuisine is known for its 'colour, aroma and taste', and Shunde cuisine is no exception. Whether the ingredients are simple or complex, a Shunde chef's craftsmanship can transform them into beautiful and gorgeous artworks. The Lunjiao Rice Cake, which is made from only glutinous rice and white sugar, is unassumingly plated side by side yet delicate in taste. The Almond and Pig Lung Soup is presented in an earthen jar filled with spices, fresh vegetables and high-quality meat bones, while aroma from the broth tickles your senses. The Pan Fried Dace is cooked with unique culinary techniques. First, raw dace meat is minced, then mixed with vegetables and

Figure 1. Lunjiao Rice Cake

Figure 2. Almond and Pig Lung Soup

Figure 3. Pan-Fried Dace

starch, and the paste is stuffed into the fish skin and then fried. The outline of the dace fish is almost unchanged, which is amazing!

From snacks to main dishes, Shunde cuisine can satisfy all the imaginations of food connoisseurs. A bowlful of milky and smooth Double-layer

Milk Custard exudes a rich sweet scent to entice the taste buds. After a bite of the fresh and tender Lunjiao Rice Cake, one cannot help but eat a few more mouthfuls. Then, nibble on a snack called Fried Glutinous Rice Balls sprinkled with sweet or salty ground peanuts and sesame seeds. Finally, slurp down a bowl of smooth hand-made Chencun Noodles, paired with pieces of refreshing braised pork.

These are just appetisers, and the main dishes are coming up. Slow-cooked in a small fire, Rice Porridge is usually eaten with fresh pork or fish, and spring onion and ginger are added for extra flavour. The smoothness of the meat complements the sweetness of the porridge. Then savour the Deep-fried Pork Rolls. Fatty and lean pork is mixed, wrapped in flour and then fried and steamed. You can't stop eating the crunchy meat rolls.

Next is the Junan Steamed Whole Pig, crispy on the outside and tender on the inside; then we have the Three-cup Chicken, which is sweet, flavourful and full of aroma; next is the golden-colour Crispy Roast Goose; and the Sautéed Water Snake Slices, which are brightly colored, fresh and fragrant, yet not too greasy. The star of the show is the dace fish. As a well-loved ingredient in Shunde, it can be cooked in many varied ways: Hand-shredded Fish Soup, Fried Fish Cake, Steamed Fish, Fish Balls, Sashimi…It can be fried, stewed, steamed and braised into cakes, balls, soups and desserts, and the choices are dizzying!

The tradition of learning and researching about food and cooking is the foundation of Shunde cuisine. It is not surprising that dishes on the banquet

Figure 4. Fried Fish Cake

Figure 5. Hand-shredded Fish Soup

Figure 6. Steamed Fish

tables are exquisite and delicious. What is valuable is that home-cooked meals in Shunde also maintain the same authenticity and taste, and the level of mastery is not compromised. Even if it is a simple dish of meat and vegetable stir-fry, the freshest vegetables and meat are used, and the home-made recipes are followed strictly. The rustic taste conveys the unique warmth and feeling of the family. 'Going home to eat' is a manifestation of the close bonds of the Shunde people. It is also this cohesive force that allows Shunde people scattered around the world to reunite. Food is not only a way of survival for the Shunde people but also a continuation of the spirit and the inheritance of culture.

With the advance of modern lifestyles, Shunde people are appreciating Western cuisine with an open and inclusive attitude. In the blend of Chinese and Western food cultures, Shunde people is fusing the spirit of traditional dishes with the goodness of Western food, gradually developing a new era of Shunde cuisine that is suitable for both Chinese and Western people, and young and old.

Flourishing food industry

In recent years, Shunde has actively participated in domestic and international food exchange activities, and has won the reputation of 'Hometown of Chinese Chefs' and 'Famous Food City'. In 2014, it was awarded the title of 'UNESCO Creative City Network — City of Gastronomy'. Taking this as an opportunity, Shunde constantly innovates and advances on its traditional food culture, and strives to create a modern food industry that integrates elements of catering, tourism, culture and media. There are currently 36 food outlets acknowledged as 'Chinese Restaurant Brand' in Shunde district, ranking top among all county-level cities in China. There are more than 13,000 catering businesses in the region, with more than 100,000 employees. The business income in 2018 is about 12.6 billion yuan. Among them, Shunfeng Group, Wumi Porridge and Baizhang Garden are not only famous for their authentic Shunde flavour, they have also expanded their businesses to other cities and regions in China.

In terms of culinary heritage and research, Shunde has 23 'Chinese Culinary Masters', 22 'Chinese Culinary Chefs', 26 'Guangdong Culinary Chefs', 19 'Guangdong Outstanding Young Cooks' and 110 'Shunde Chefs'. From 2011 to 2013, three batches of representative Shunde cuisine and the English translation of 94 Shunde dishes were announced. In 2012, the Shunfeng Culinary Institute at UCSI University in Malaysia was established, and Shunde's culinary training business began to spread overseas. In 2014, the Chinese Culinary Institute officially opened in the Shunde Vocational and Technical College to promote professional chef training and industry research.

In terms of branding, the Shunde District Tourism Bureau combines traditional folk activities with Shunde cuisine to develop unique 'flower banquets' and 'maid cuisine' to give Shunde cuisine a new twist. After several rounds of food culture seminars and demonstrations, the characteristics of Shunde's food culture are finally defined as 'five flavours, six arts, fresh drinks, good food and natural ingredients', which is concise and meaningful. In addition, the Tourism Bureau also plans to launch a series of brochures, such as 'Guide to Shunde Cuisine', 'Sentimental Shunde', 'Gourmet Style' and 'Walking around Shunde for Gourmet', which fully record the development process of Shunde cuisine and also promote the development of Shunde food culture towards integration and systematisation.

In the era of the integration of traditional and new media, the Shunde people know how to meet this trend. On the one hand, they actively cooperate with well-known domestic and foreign TV media to produce popular documentary films and variety shows such as 'A Bite of Shunde', 'A Taste of China', 'The Story of the Eels' and so on. At the same time, Shunde also promotes these shows on the new media platform by driving up online traffic and enhancing interaction with the audience, so as to promote the Shunde food culture. Especially after the documentary 'A Bite of Shunde' was broadcast, the yearly online visitors reached 2 billion people, setting off a wave of domestic and foreign diners travelling to Shunde to 'seek the taste of Shunde', which drove the development of the local tourism/catering industry.

Also, as a famous hometown of overseas Chinese, Shunde has not forgotten to promote its food culture while attending to overseas Chinese affairs. During the 2016 Shunde Worldwide Friendship Association meetings, Shunde launched a special food promotion event for more than 1,000 Shunde folks from more than 20 countries and regions. Using the platform of economic and trade cooperation, Shunde also conducts food promotion,

Figure 7. Variety Show - 'A Bite of Shunde'

cooking demonstrations and other activities in Canada, South Africa, Germany, Singapore, Malaysia and other countries.

In terms of hardware and facilities construction, the Shunde International Food Culture Exchange Centre, undertaken by the Shunde District Tourism Bureau, is expected to be opened in 2019. The project covers an area of about 2,500 square metres and includes many functions such as food culture display, cooking performances, conferences, etc. It is expected to become an important platform for Shunde's food industry.

Shunde Food Festival

Since 2006, Shunde has successfully organised thirteen annual Food Culture Festival (formally renamed in 2015 as World's Food Capital — Shunde Food Festival). The event is centred on a food show held during China's National Day and lasts for nearly half a year. It consists of a series of activities such as culinary competitions, food shows, and tourist food tastings. During the event, people from all walks of life, such as the native people, tourists, media, and catering industry practitioners were brought together to share food, chat about culture and compare cooking.

Figure 8. The 2018 Shunde Food Festival

With the active promotion and enthusiastic participation of the government, residents, enterprises, media and other parties, the Shunde Food Festival has made a name for itself, becoming a unique and shining representative of Shunde. In 2018, the varied themes of the Food Festival, such as 'Finding Shunde', 'One Belt and One Road' and 'International Cuisine' were oriented to the market and closely followed the trends of the times. In just five days, it attracted more than 1.1 million participants and achieved more than 40 million yuan in sales.

The participation of towns and streets, the linkage of industry and festivals, and the market-oriented operation are important components for the Shunde Food Festival and the festival gradually become larger and more established. The participation of the various towns and streets has ignited the enthusiasm of the residents in partaking in the celebrations.

The establishment of events at the towns and streets not only adds colour to the festivities but also provides a rare opportunity for the grassroots culture to be exhibited for all to see. The Food Festival is also giving a fillip to the standardisation of Shunde cuisine, accelerating the pace of regional tourism and catering industry upgrades, and consolidating Shunde's leading position in the national food industry. In the early stage of the Food Festival, the government was the organiser. After attracting and maintaining many participants and encouraging the business community and the media to join, the Food Festival has now become a market-oriented operation. In recent years, well-known enterprises such as Midea, OCT, Macro and Haitian have joined the event in the form of title sponsors and sponsorships. On the one hand, they have achieved good advertisement through the platform, and on the other hand, they have saved fiscal expenditures for the local government. It also encourages more enterprises to participate in the events and is a model for cooperation between government and business.

UNESCO City of Gastronomy

In 2014, Shunde officially became a member of the UNESCO Creative City Network — City of Gastronomy, and actively participated in related activities organised by the network. Shunde was frequently invited to share its development experiences at international conferences, and Shunde cuisine was promoted around the world. In 2016, Shunde was invited to present the development of its strong food brand and to showcase the influence of Shunde city at the Macau International Food Forum. In the same year, at the Beijing summit of UNESCO Creative City Network, Shunde presented the report 'The Power of Food — The Role of Creativity in Cities in the Belt and Road Initiative'. This report once again showed the world the open and inclusive nature of Shunde. In 2017, Shunde was the only Chinese city to be invited to share its achievements and experience as a food capital at the 10th Summit of UNESCO Creative City Network.

Shunde is also actively participating in activities between cities in the Creative City Network and looking for cooperation opportunities. On the one hand, Shunde participated in food tours to Parma in Italy, Jeonju in South Korea, Macau, Thailand, Spain, Brazil and other cities. On the other hand, mayors of cities in the Network were invited to visit Shunde. In 2018, during the visit by the Turkish representative, the international cooperation project 'The Food Culture of the Silk Road' was launched. It was supported by the Shunde government and other Network member cities.

Conclusion

Excellent natural conditions and a developed regional economy are the sources of nourishment for Shunde's food culture. Under the skillful hands of the Shunde people, ordinary ingredients can be turned into delicious works of art in food. Food also conveys the beautiful hopes of the Shunde people who love life, respect historical traditions and have a strong sense of belonging to their ancestral roots. In the process of inheriting and promoting the food culture of Shunde, Shunde has skillfully integrated the elements of food, culture, education and training to create a unique and beautiful Shunde food industry. They have also actively promoted Shunde cuisine by participating in international exchanges and cooperation.

Chapter 5

Shunde's Celebrities

The Chinese reform and opening up and the globalisation drive in the 1980s provided twin external drives to the monumental success of Shunde. People in Shunde are determined, bold, indomitable, and adaptable; to build Shunde's story, they are able to seize once-in-a-lifetime fleeting opportunities. This article selects various respected Shunde celebrities from the business, social development, history and cultural sectors, extrapolating their stories to reflect on Shunde's story and its contribution towards China's development.

Shunde Tai-pan

Shunde has centuries worth of experience in agriculture and trading. The people are courageous, have steady perseverance and possess strong business sense. Many Shunde locals moved to Hong Kong and Macau in the 20th century and successfully built their business empires. Shunde natives have a tradition of philanthropy and often set up charity institutions such as hospitals, nursing homes and schools to help their hometown after their success.

Leung Kau-Kui (1903–1994): Hong Kong tai-pan and philanthropist

Leung Kau-Kui was born into a businessman's family at Beitou Village, Xingtan Town, Shunde. At a young age, Leung followed his father to

Guangzhou. He became an apprentice at a small credit union, eventually opening his own (Hoi Hing Credit Union). When World War II broke out, Leung moved his Guangzhou and Hong Kong operations to the neutral territory of Macau, his business acumen sparing his company from damages brought by the war. He established Tai Fong Credit Union with other Guangdong businesspeople and set up a branch in Guangzhou Bay (present-day Zhanjiang City). Taking advantage of the goods shortage problem during the war, he built his fortune by establishing a strong trading operation based in Macau and the surrounding Guangzhou Bay area.

Sensing the central role that Hong Kong is going to play in the China coastal trade after the Chinese civil war, Leung moved to Hong Kong and established Dah Chong Hong in 1949. To solve the acute foreign exchange shortage problem after the establishment of the People's Republic of China, he embarked on barter trade to help his mainland customers and successfully built a trading network connecting Hong Kong, Guangzhou and Hankou, mainly covering Southern China. His business flourished, and he later expanded into banking with the Hang Seng Bank. In 1964, The Hong Kong & Shanghai Banking Corporation (HSBC) took over the majority stake of Hang Seng Bank and Leung became a junior business partner of the renowned Hong Kong Bank group.

Leung was an avid philanthropist and considered one of the top ten philanthropists in Hong Kong. He held firmly to the belief that material wealth, which was obtained from society, should also be used for the benefit of the society and its people. When he became successful, he followed the tradition of helping his hometown and contributed significantly to Shunde's social infrastructure development. His contribution started from the late 1970s. Xingtan Beitou Town Hall, Beitou Primary School, Xingtan Liangzhu Middle School, Shunde Liangzhu Library and many other projects were made possible through Leung's donation. In 1988, Leung donated 5.5 million Hong Kong dollars and collaborated with the Shunde district government to establish an integrated middle school with both vocational and regular courses — Shunde Leung Kau-Kui Middle School. The middle school later upgraded to become Shunde Leung Kau-Kui Technical School, the primary institution in Shunde catered to high-school level technical training. To support the development of local Shunde businesses, Leung also donated 5 million Hong Kong dollars to establish the Shunde Leung Kau-Kui

Welfare Foundation, which promotes domestic NGO welfare work. Over the years, Leung donated more than 40 million Hong Kong dollars to his hometown, selflessly paving the way for the future generation. He is a classic example of successful Chinese businessmen showing patriotism for their country and hometown.

Cheng Yu-Tung (1925–2016): *Visionary Jewellery King*

Cheng Yu-Tung came from Lunjiao Town, Shunde. He was the Chairman of Hong Kong New World Development Co., Ltd. and Hong Kong Chow Tai Fook Jewellery Co., Ltd., Vice-Chairman of Hong Kong Real Estate Developers Association, Director of Hong Kong Hang Seng Bank. He was also Honorary President of the Hong Kong-Shunde Friendship Association and Shunde Worldwide Friendship Association.

Cheng came from a family in the textile trade. His father, Zheng Jingyi, taught Cheng how to be ambitious and diligent. Cheng left his hometown alone and went to work at Macau. He worked as a goldsmith apprentice in Chow Tai Fook Jewellery Shop, owned by the namesake of the company and his fellow villager, Chow Tai Fook. Cheng's competence, talent and honesty won the heart of Chow, and he eventually married Ms Zhou Cuiying, the daughter of Chow Tai Fook. Cheng's business acumen and ambition drove the expansion of the company, and he became one of the industry's leading figure in the 1950s. He later acquired majority shareholding of Chow Tai Fook Jewellery from his retired father-in-law and other shareholders to become its major shareholder.

Cheng was a pragmatic businessman with good business acumen. Under his leadership, Chow Tai Fook Jewellery became a limited company, and its business accelerated, spreading to Hong Kong and Macau. He pioneered the first '999.9' gold bar trading in Hong Kong, and the jewellery business extended to South Asia, Belgium, the United Kingdom and the United States. He also built a diamond-cutting factory in South Africa. The developments made the company Hong Kong's largest diamond dealer, earning it the title of Southeast Asia's 'Jewel King'. Chow Tai Fook Jewellery listed in Hong Kong in 2011 and is the largest jewellery company in the world today. It has a market capitalisation of more than 10 billion US dollars.

The 1967 Hong Kong riots saw many wealthy people dumping real estate properties at a bargain price. Cheng, however, saw it as an opportunity to buy land cheaply and therefore invested heavily in real estate. In 1970, he established New World Development Co., Ltd. with his close friends and diversified into hotels, communications, energy, transportation infrastructure, department stores and other businesses. New World Development is a major conglomerate in Hong Kong and its investment covers not only Hong Kong and China, but also in countries like the United Kingdom, the United States, and in Southeast Asia.

Cheng's goal in life was to help society. He often said that 'I make my fortune from society, and I want to repay the grace given to me by spending it to benefit the society'. Although Cheng left his hometown at a young age, he remained deeply attached to his roots. As early as 1978, he donated 1.8 million Hong Kong dollars to expand Shunde Huaqiao Middle School and set up a scholarship fund in memory of his father. He give 80 million yuan to build the Cheng Yu-Tung Middle School in Shunde in 1994. In 2004, he donated 15 million Hong Kong dollars and rallied his family members to put in 500 thousand Hong Kong dollars to build Zheng Jing Yi Vocational School.

Since China's reform and opening up, Cheng's total donation to Shunde reached 190 million yuan. Not only that, Cheng also actively supported Shunde's economic development. Over the years, he set up a jewellery processing factory in Lunjiao Town as well as the New World Hotel in Shunde, established a partnership to build a lime sand brick factory, and had many other projects. Shunde's success as the jewellery manufacturing centre of Southern China can be attributed to his investment.

Lee Shau-Kee (1928–): Real estate magnate and renowned 'Warren Buffet of Asia'

Lee Shau-Kee is born to a wealthy merchant family in Shunde and well versed in the traditional Chinese classics — Four Books and Five Classics. At the tender age of six, his father arranged for him to stay in his family's shop to learn how to do business. Lee was good in mental arithmetic, and his business acumen showed at a young age. By the time he was 12, he was asked by his father to run the family shop. At 20, Lee went to Hong Kong alone with just 1,000 yuan in his pocket, and he managed to strike his first fortune dealing in foreign exchange and gold.

The horrifying experience of war convinced him that the only asset that could withstand the test of time was real estate. After he built his fortune, he formed Yongye Co., Ltd with seven partners. It was a real estate company which built houses for the lower- and middle-income families, sold in instalments. The affordable properties soon sold out. After Yongye's success, he and his partners restructured the company and formed a new company — Sun Hung Kai & Co. Ltd. Lee became its general manager and took charge of property design, land acquisition and sales. His innovative approach and perseverance not only enabled the company to quickly become Hong Kong's leading real estate company but also earned him the title 'King of Real Estate'. In 1975, Lee set up his own company, Henderson Land Development Co., Ltd., and began dealing with the stock market. He later used methods like back door listing and leverage to acquire more prominent companies, realising and accumulating a mass amount of wealth. He earned the nickname 'Warren Buffet of Asia' along the way.

Lee is passionate about education and has sponsored more than 400 education projects in the mainland since 1982. In 1978, he supported the Hong Kong-Shunde Friendship Association and founded the Shunde Friendship Association Lee Shau-Kee Middle School. Together with Dr Cheng Yu-Tung, a total of 1.8 million yuan was donated to expand Shunde Huaqiao Middle School, 3.1 million Hong Kong dollars to build Shunde Hospital, and 5 million Hong Kong dollars to build Shunde Sports Centre. In 1994, 80 million yuan was donated to build Shunde Lee Shau-Kee Middle School. Lee's charitable projects are all over China and cover many aspects of society like education, training and housing.

Other world-renowned celebrities from Shunde

Bruce Lee (1940–1973): *Legendary martial arts master*

Bruce Lee was born 'Lee Zhen Fan' in San Francisco. His ancestors came from Shunde. He was an international martial artist, instructor and philosopher who popularised Chinese martial arts (otherwise known as Chinese Kung Fu) to the world in the 1970s through films. He lived in Hong Kong during his childhood and was a martial arts student of Ip Man, a renowned Chinese martial arts guru of the Wing Chun school. He migrated to the United States to study and opened a martial arts dojo in California at the age of 18. He then began to appear in a TV series as a guest performer and worked hard to change the western onscreen stereotype that Asians were weak and easily bullied.

In 1970, Lee went back to Hong Kong to star in the film 'The Big Boss'. The opportunity opened doors for him, and he was later invited to star in 'Fist of Fury', 'The Way of the Dragon', 'Enter the Dragon' and other films that were new to the international film industry. He popularised many oriental martial arts forms like Jeet Kune Do, One Inch Punch and Nunchaku and is the first Chinese movie personality that achieved global acclaim. In 1973, Lee died in a mysterious accident in Hong Kong when he was only 33 years old. In 1993, the United States issued commemorative banknotes for Lee's 20th death anniversary. During the same year, he was honoured a star on the Hollywood Walk of Fame and given the 'Lifetime Achievement Award' by the Hong Kong Film Awards. In 1998, the Chinese Wushu Association posthumously awarded Lee the 'Martial Arts Movie Superstar Award'.

Lee's ancestral home is in Shangcun Township, Junan Town, Shunde. It was built by his grandfather Lee Jun-biu and housed two generations of Lee's — his grandfather as well as his father. The alley where the home is located is now named 'Xiaolong Alley', after Bruce Lee's professional Chinese name. To commemorate Lee, a Bruce Lee theme park was built near the ancestral home, showcasing Lee's martial arts and performing arts career, as well as his life and family history.

Margaret Chan Fung Fu-chun (1947–): First Chinese Woman to become Director-General of WHO

Born in Hong Kong, Margaret Chan Fung Fu-chun's ancestral home is Leliu, Shunde. From 1973 to 1977, Chan studied for a medical degree from the University of Western Ontario, Canada. After graduation, she joined the Hong Kong Department of Health as a doctor. In 1985, Chan attained a master's degree in public health from the National University of Singapore, and in 1994 became the first female director in the Hong Kong Department of Health. Chan was appointed as Director of the World Health Organisation

(WHO) Human Environmental Protection Agency in 2003. Her primary responsibility was to prevent and control infectious disease, which she did exceptionally well and won the accolades of many countries. In 2005, Chan served as both Director of Infectious Diseases Monitoring and Response Bureau as well as Director-General of the WHO. In 2006, she became Director-General of WHO with the highest vote on record. She was subsequently re-elected from 2012 to 2017. In 2017, Chan stepped down from her post.

Foreign dignitaries with Shunde ancestry

Sir James Richard Marie Mancham (1939–2017):
First President of Seychelles

Sir James Mancham was the first President of the Republic of Seychelles from 1976 to 1977. He carries ancestry from different races, and his grandfather was from Lecong, Shunde. His Chinese name was Chen Wen Jin. In 2014 Sir James went back to China to trace his root. During the trip, he reunited with long-lost relatives and rebuilt his connection with them, paid homage to the ancestral temple and renewed his tie with Shunde.

Monique Agnes Ohsan Bellepeau (1942–):
Former Vice-President of Mauritius

Ohsan Bellepeau was the first female Vice-President of Mauritius. Her ancestors came from Lecong, Shunde. From 1965 to 1967, Ohsan Bellepeau served as a news broadcaster in the Mauritius Broadcasting Corporation. She later became a businesswoman after her marriage. In 1990 she joined the Chamber of Commerce and the Labour Party, subsequently becoming an executive board member of the Party. In 1995 she served as a member of parliament, from 1997 to 2000 Minister of Urban and Rural Development, from 2007 to 2010 Chairman of the Labour Party, and from 2010 to 2016 Vice-President of Mauritius.

Ohsan Bellepeau's grandfather moved from Lecong, Shunde to Mauritius at the turn of the twentieth century. There he married a local Mauritius wife, built a family, and settled down. Her father was born in Mauritius, but due to his early death, Bellepeau grew up under the care of her uncle, who was proficient in Chinese poetry and paintings. The hobby of her uncle fed her curiosity and yearning towards her Shunde hometown. In 2008, her uncle wrote a letter detailing their family's root and solicited help from the Mauritius embassy and Shunde's Overseas Chinese Affairs Department. Ohsan Bellepeau eventually succeeded in locating her relatives in Shunde and returned to Lecong to reunite with her distant relatives during a 2013 China visit. After the family reunion, she exclaimed that she would bring her grandchildren in the future so that they may interact with their extended family and know their roots. In July 2014, Ohsan Bellepeau went to London to attend the ninth Shunde Worldwide Friendship Association conference, showing her emotional attachment to Shunde.

Conclusion

The spirit of perseverance, courage and determination are traditional values defining Shunde people no matter where they are. Their strong character allowed them to make their mark in China and the rest of the world, expanding footprints, building business empires and fulfilling destinies. At the same time, strong clan spirit remains a strong impetus for overseas Shunde children to reconnect with their roots, find a spiritual home and contribute back regardless of challenges they may face along the way. The indomitable Shunde value and spirit will undoubtedly bring more success to Shunde, China and the world in the future.

Part 2
Deciphering Shunde's Success: Reform & Innovation

Chapter 6

The Shunde Economic Phenomenon

Since China's reform and opening up started in 1978, Shunde has transformed from a productive agricultural region into one of the important members of the Pearl River Delta — the world's factory. Before the reform and opening up, Shunde was not well known in China. Historically, Shunde was a rich agricultural area in Guangdong, boasting a cultural atmosphere and spawning many wealthy overseas Chinese. At the same time, Shunde is also a famous culinary capital in southern China. A popular saying goes, 'Eat at Guangzhou, but the cook must be from Fengcheng (the old name of Shunde)' — such is the esteem for Shunde cuisine.

The reform and opening up in 1978 changed the historical destiny of Shunde. The pioneering spirit of its people made Shunde a nationally recognised reform forerunner in the 1980s and 1990s. From 1978 to 2017, the population of the district increased from 780,000 to more than 2.6 million, and the regional GDP increased from 475 million yuan to 301.6 billion yuan. In the 40 years of reform and opening up, the nominal GDP of the district has increased by 634 times, and the population has also increased by more than three times. In the past 40 years, the per capita GDP has risen from 612 yuan to nearly 119,000 yuan, a remarkable 200-fold growth, which is higher than the 155-fold increase of 385 yuan to 59,660 yuan of the country.

In 2017, the per capita nominal GDP of Shunde was 119,000 yuan — equivalent to more than 18,000 US dollars, far exceeding the 12,000 US dollars per capita nominal GDP defined by the World Bank as acheiving

Table 1. Population and income data of Shunde

Year	GDP (million yuan)	Household registration population (thousand people)	Total number of residents (thousand people)	Per capita GDP (yuan)	Disposable income of urban residents (yuan)	Disposable income of rural residents (yuan)
1978	475	781				
1980	529	529				
1985	1503	848				
1990	4419	918	973		3377	1854
1995	16960	1009	1288			
2000	36459	1081	1695	22213	14394	6646
2005	82512	1163	1955	51127	24455	26433
2010	178917	1225	2463	74420	30618	12543
2015	258668	1284	2535	102538	42259	26860
2017	305930	1393	2615	1116915	49881	31918

developed country status. Shunde has now firmly entered the ranks of economically developed regions.

Shunde's remarkable achievements in economic and social development have enabled it to be ranked first among China's top 100 cities/jurisdictions with comprehensive strength for seven consecutive years. It has also been listed ten times as one of China's top 10 well-off demonstration cities and counties.

Government reforms have created the Shunde economic phenomenon of today

Shunde made two outstanding contributions to China's reforms in the 1980s and 1990s. First, in the 1980s, Shunde's pragmatic and enterprising people pioneered a government-led development model based on town and village-based collective ownership and created some of the first 'three-plus-one' enterprises. The 'Shunde Model' is based on the development of township enterprises, enabling Shunde to become the first among the 'Four Tiger Cubs of Guangdong'.

Before China's reform and opening up, the commune system in the agricultural planned economy dictated that all agricultural harvests belonged to the communes; the farmers were compensated with farm products according to work done, and the farm products could not be bought and sold freely. The enterprising spirit of the farmers was suppressed.

Under the industrial planned economy, state-owned enterprises controlled major production resources, these enterprises were ran by government departments, and small services and businesses were collectively owned by villages and towns. All large, medium and small production units were either state- or collectively-owned. There was no need for an individual's entrepreneurship, and productivity was low.

The reforms that began in 1978 allowed farmers to lease land from the villages, considerably boosting rural productivity. At the same time, the reforms enabled many farmers to leave farming behind to join the vast labour force needed for emerging light industries. The government began to allow individuals to set up township enterprises to engage in light industrial manufacturing or other activities to absorb labour force from the remaining agricultural population.

In the Guangdong model, the village or town was nominally the owner of the township enterprise, and the investors only needed to pay a certain fee to the township. The operation and finance of the enterprise were controlled by the investors, which created the conditions for the emergence of private enterprises. The Guangdong model was different from the Sunan model in which the villages and towns collectively funded the operation of township enterprises and retained actual ownership.

The Guangdong model not only retained the legal and social framework of the collective economy but also introduced the efficiency and flexibility of private enterprise, thereby injecting vitality into the Chinese economy that had just started to reform.

In the early 1980s, Shunde became the pioneer of the township model of Guangdong enterprises. Shunde adopted an open and encouraging attitude towards the establishment of township and village enterprises and successfully absorbed the surplus rural labour force after the reform of the agricultural sector. This Lewis labour transfer mechanism not only provided cheap labour for emerging labour-intensive industries but also significantly increased the local GDP. It also encouraged aspiring local entrepreneurs to invest in their own personally managed township enterprises.

At the same time, Shunde actively supported the emerging 'three-plus-one' model for export processing, and the emerging township enterprises were mostly concentrated on the exports business. Under the 'three-plus-one' system, Shunde's township enterprises carried out materials processing, sample processing, and assembly of parts. Overseas suppliers provided free imported machinery and technology to compensate for the processing labour. The model addressed the problems of shortage of equipment, technology and capital for the township and village enterprises in the early stages of economic development. Shunde set up one of the first 'three-plus-one' enterprises in the apparel industry. It quickly became an vital compensation trade centre by cooperating with Hong Kong, one of the world's largest garment exporting outlets. Shunde Dajin Clothing Factory was one of the first township enterprises in China to engage in the 'three-plus-one' compensation trade. The success of Shunde's economy in the 1980s earned it the moniker 'Shunde model'. The average annual GDP growth rate of Shunde in the 1980s was 22.3%.

In the 1990s, Shunde made an important contribution to China's reform and opening up for a second time. At that time, China had opened a new round of reforms after Deng Xiaoping's famous Southern Tour in 1992. In the same year, Shunde was selected as the comprehensive reform pilot county of Guangdong province. The Guangdong provincial government supported Shunde to promote comprehensive reforms, emphasising on the reform of the administrative management system and the reform of property rights system. Shunde grasped this historical opportunity and advanced the change of the property rights system, established a new socialist market economy, and became the forerunner of China's economic reform.

The transformation of state-owned enterprises and the reorganisation of property rights of township and village enterprises benefited managers and investors, and the efficiency of enterprises increased substantially. Shunde's two largest private companies, Midea and Country Garden, were established in the 1990s and they achieved sales of more than 200 billion yuan in 2017. Many of Shunde's 'invisible champions' were also products of the market-oriented reforms. The reforms of the 1990s laid the basis for Shunde's private enterprise-led economic model. Shunde's average annual GDP growth rate in the 1990s was 25.5%.

Shunde's reform successes in the 1980s and 1990s cemented its high-ranking position in the history of China's reform. In the process, Shunde cultivated cadres and entrepreneurs at all levels who were highly adaptable and able to implement reforms and changes, making the district an important pilot for China's reform. In 2009, Shunde was selected by the Guangdong provincial government for a series of comprehensive reforms focusing on the social system and grassroots governance. In 2018, Shunde was approved to be the pilot zone for the reform and innovation of a high-quality development system in Guangdong province.

Shunde's economy is based on manufacturing

Shunde created a manufacturing-based economic system in the 1980s which continues to exist today. The district government and the business community have never wavered in their backing for the manufacturing industry. The district government has made a series of policies to support and guide the transformation and upgrading of the manufacturing industry, while corporate investment and scientific research investment are also heavily concentrated in manufacturing. The district government is currently running the 'Technology Shunde' programme, aiming at the upgrading of traditional manufacturing industries through research & development.

The value-added of Shunde's industrial output value has consistently remained above 55% of GDP. In 2017, the first, second and third industrial structure of Shunde were 1.5%: 56.3%: and 42.3% respectively. As of February 2018, there were 25,381 industrial enterprises in the district, including 1,726 enterprises with an annual output value of 20 million yuan.

Shunde has formed eight pillar industries — household appliances, machinery and equipment, information and communications technology, textiles and garments, fine chemicals, packaging and printing, furniture manufacturing, and medicine and health care. In 2017, the industrial output value of the eight pillar industries accounted for 77.8% of the industrial output value of enterprises above a designated size. Household appliances and machinery and equipment are the leading industries in Shunde, with output values of more than 200 billion yuan. In recent years, three newly emerging major industries — jewellery, automobile parts, and lighting equipment — have also been developing rapidly. The government is currently encouraging the development of several emerging industries, including smart manufacturing, industrial design, e-commerce, and conferences and exhibitions.

Sophisticated industrial clusters and highly localised products

Before the reform and opening up, Shunde was an agricultural district with a fledgling industrial base. Most of Guangdong province's industrial investment was concentrated in neighbouring Guangzhou. The main ways for Shunde's town and village enterprises to acquire production technology in the 1980s were through industrial clusters, industry associations, and other private channels. These informal setups facilitated information and technical exchanges.

The industrial cluster network, comprising of vertical and horizontal pathways, increases the professionalism of enterprises, improves quality, and spreads risks, and as such, it can establish an industrial ecology with a, healthy competitive spirit. At the same time, it also enhances the level of product localisation, effectively reduces product costs, and benefits production by means of short turnaround time and fast technology updates.

The key characteristics of Shunde's main industrial clusters are as follow:

1. Household Appliances: It is the most important industry in Shunde, and it produces mainly white goods. It has a large volume and a wide range of products. It also has a complete industrial chain, with more than 3,200 home appliances manufacturers and supporting enterprises. The industry accounts for 15% of the country's household appliances industry and enjoys the reputation of being 'the capital of Chinese home appliances'. There are three main advantages enjoyed by the household appliances industry: first, the high concentration of enterprises and a healthy competitive spirit; second, reasonable structure and coordinated development of large and medium-sized enterprises; finally, a large number of brands and high brand recognition.
2. Machinery and Equipment: Shunde's machinery and equipment industry has grown in tandem with the household appliances and furniture manufacturing industries. Shunde has become the country's largest air-conditioning compressor production base and the country's largest woodworking machinery manufacturing and sales base. With the transformation and upgrading of manufacturing industries in Shunde and southern China, Shunde's machinery and equipment industry has maintained a double-digit growth rate for the past five years. Sub-sector

industries such as industrial equipment, industrial robots, intelligent manufacturing and automobile parts are developing rapidly.

3. Furniture Manufacturing: There are 16,376 enterprises involved in furniture-related industries in Shunde, including about 5,000 furniture manufacturing enterprises. Longjiang is 'the capital of Chinese furniture manufacturing' and is China's largest raw material production and distribution centre and the largest furniture material market. Lecong is 'the capital of Chinese furniture trade' and has an extensive influence on the world furniture industry. Shunde's furniture manufacturing cluster is the most comprehensivefurniture industrial cluster in China's supply chain system.

4. Fine Chemicals: Shunde is the 'hometown of Chinese coatings'. There are about 150 coating companies in the district, mainly in furniture coatings and architectural coatings. Furniture coatings enterprises account for about 50% of the industry, while architectural coatings enterprises account for about 40%. Shunde's fine chemical industry has grown steadily alongside the furniture manufacturing industry.

5. Information and Communications Technology: Shunde's ICT industry focuses on the production of whole machines with Lunjiao as the core, and also the production of small household appliances and electronic components and spare parts with Daliang and Leliu as the core. More than 90% of the components required by Shunde's ICT enterprises can be procured locally in the district.

6. Textiles and Apparel: There are more than 3,000 textile and garment production enterprises in the district, ranging from textiles, fabrics, printing and dyeing to clothing and apparel, etc. There are many clusters in this industry, such as the Junan Denim Industry Group, the Xingtan Printing and Dyeing Industry Group, and the Lunjiao Gambiered Guangzhou Gauze Industry Group.

7. Hardware: Leliu in Shunde has three honours to its name: 'the capital of Chinese Home Hardware', 'the capital of Chinese hinges' and 'the capital of Chinese sliding rails', and is the largest home hardware industry cluster in China. At present, Leliu has 1,200 hardware and spare parts manufacturing enterprises.

8. Lighting: Leliu is also one of the places in China with the highest concentration of domestic lighting manufacturers. It has nearly 1,000

lighting fixtures enterprises and related supporting enterprises, accounting for 60% of the domestic commercial lighting output value.
9. E-commerce: Shunde has more than 10,000 online merchants engaged in B2C and B2B transactions, more than 15 e-commerce platforms, and nearly 20 e-commerce industry parks under construction. Among them, Longjiang Furniture Industry Park has been recognised as an e-commerce demonstration base by the Ministry of Commerce; Europol Intelligent Network, Midea Group's e-commerce and Flying Fish have been recognised as national e-commerce demonstration enterprises by the Ministry of Commerce. Shunde has 25 enterprises listed as the provincial top 100 e-commerce enterprises, ranking second in the province. It also has a total of 118 e-commerce demonstration enterprises. Shunde and other manufacturing industry bases in the Pearl River Delta provide a wide range of goods for e-commerce. Shunde's home appliances, furniture, home decor, food, steel, plastics, hardware and building materials, machinery, and denim industries are all expanding their businesses through the new e-commerce channels.

These industrial clusters have consolidated the position of Shunde's manufacturing industry in the market. In 2017, the export value of the whole district was 138.3 billion yuan, and the import value was 38.1 billion yuan. Such a vast trade surplus highlights the advantage of maintaining a high level of localisation in Shunde's products.

The international market: Brand building and quality assurance

In the early days of reform and opening up, Shunde's entrepreneurs took the lead in entering the international market through the 'three-plus-one' model. They recognised the difficulties of production and quality control of products to be sold overseas, and also realised the importance of brand building. Shunde had ten years' prior experience than the rest of China in the area of light industrial manufacturing with products that are of international standards. This first-mover advantage played a vital role in the subsequent establishment of the Shunde brand. As at the end of 2016, Shunde had 34 well-known national trademarks, 151 famous Guangdong province branded products and 146 famous Guangdong province trademarks. In the international market, 'Made in Shunde' is a valuable business card.

Industry dominated by private enterprises: Quick response to the market

Shunde's private enterprises occupy a dominant position in the manufacturing industry. In 2017, private enterprises accounted for more than 77% of industrial production, contributing 80.89% to the industrial growth of the district. In 2015, China's overall exports fell, yet Shunde's exports remained stable. GDP growth in Shunde has consistently been higher than the national level in the same period. These data show that private enterprises have relatively efficient adaptability to market changes. The Chinese government has recently launched a series of policies to support private enterprises, thereby affirming the critical position of private enterprises in the development of the market economy.

Conclusion

With its wealth of experience gleaned from economic development, Shunde has numerous assets — such as deep level of marketisation, high degree of industrial clustering, high localisation of products, flexible private enterprises, and a cooperative relationship between the government and enterprises — to offer to the future development of the Guangdong-Hong Kong-Macau Greater Bay Area. Several of Shunde's pillar manufacturing industries have low overlap with other Greater Bay Area industries. With further integration of the Greater Bay Area economy and the subsequent expansion of regional cooperation, Shunde's industrial clusters will benefit significantly from industrial upgrading. The role of Shunde in the Greater Bay Area will be analysed in another article.

Chapter 7

Shunde and the World Economy

In a span of 40 years from 1978, Shunde successfully transformed itself from an agricultural society to become a key manufacturing centre in Southern China. The transformation of Shunde reflected the successful integration of China into the global economic system. The transformation of Shunde's town and village enterprises (TVEs) into global manufacturing giants today is not an easy process and is worth studying. This article reviews the growth story of Shunde and its integration into the global economy.

Before China's 1978 reform and opening up

Shunde is endowed with favourable natural resources, and its agricultural economy is cash-crop based. Historically, it is famous for its silk and aquaculture industry. A good number of its people worked as petty traders and workers rather than traditional subsistence farmers in the past; hence Shunde's society was already familiar with the operation of market-based economics before the 1978 reform and opening up. There were some agricultural-based industries before 1978.

Before the reform and opening up, peasants were tied to the planned economy of the state and bound to the land. They had little incentive to work hard and had no power to make personal decisions on what jobs to take. At the same time, the state-mandated price gaps between industrial and agricultural products were widening in favour of the industrial sector. Farmers were not able to obtain the necessary funding to develop rural industries. Up until 1978, Shunde had only 214 manufacturing businesses, mainly engaged in activities supporting the agricultural sectors such as bamboo ware workshop, wood machinery manufacturing, tractor repair and maintenance, etc. The industrial output value was only 847 million yuan, typical of an agricultural society.

At that time, Shunde industrial talents faced a 'one — too little, two — very low, three — very old' (一少、两低、三老) predicament. 'One — too little' refers to the small number of professionals working in the industrial sector; Shunde had fewer than 10,000 professionals, and they were concentrated in educational institutions, medical clinics, and state-owned enterprises (SOEs). There were only 51 professional technicians and engineers in the industrial sector. 'Two — very low' refers to the low level of professional qualifications of the engineers. The entire Shunde county did not have a single engineer who graduated from university. Out of the 51 engineering professionals, 14 graduated from polytechnics while 37 graduated from technical schools. 'Three — very old' means that the technological know-how of all the 51 industrial professionals was old and outdated.

In a nutshell, before China's reform and opening up, Shunde lacked funds, skills, and technology to develop the manufacturing sector.

Rongqi Dajin Clothing Factory

In August 1978, Shunde's Rongqi Town and Hong Kong's Dajin Co., Ltd. set up a garment factory called Rongqi Dajin Clothing Factory (容奇大进制衣厂). (Later in 2000, Rongqi Town and Guizhou Town merged to form today's Ronggui town.) The Hong Kong partner provided capital investment, equipment, technology, management, raw materials and export orders, while the factory provided local labour to work on the export orders.

Dajin Clothing Factory was China's first group of TVEs to engage in the compensation trade export model. In the model, the foreign partner brings in raw materials, machinery and technology, while the local partner provides labour and factory space to make the products specified by the foreign partner. The foreign partner buys all the finished products, and its input is compensated by the labour component of the product.

The original contract period for Dajin Clothing Factory was six years. The factory's business model was quite successful; in its first year of operation, the small factory of 300 workers earned 200,000 US dollars in net income.

By 1983, the company successfully paid back all its obligations to the Hong Kong partner one year ahead of the original contract terms, learnt all the production techniques and became an independent TVE of Rongqi Town.

In short, Rongqi Dajin Clothing Factory spearheaded the country in adopting the compensation trade export model and integrating it into the global trading system.

Complementary reforms in the 1980s

The success of Dajin Clothing Factory created the Dajin Effect and caused the proliferation of compensation trade-based TVEs. On the one hand, the government took loans and built extensive physical infrastructure in transportation and telecommunications to facilitate the operation of new TVEs. On the other hand, incentives were implemented to entice foreign investors and local governments to set up export-oriented TVEs. 1987 saw the establishment of 548 compensation trade businesses, the most since the model was started by Dajin in 1978. Labour income from the compensation trade hit 7 million US dollars that year.

In 1983, there were 2,019 TVEs with a total output value of 610 million yuan. The number of TVEs increased a whooping 8.3 times and output value increased 1.93 times compared to 1978. The TVEs' output value accounted for 40% of the county's 1.53 billion yuan industrial and agricultural output value, and 50% of the county's industrial output value. 1983 was the year when TVEs became an indispensable part of the county's industrial development. The rapid growth of TVEs within five years reflected the courage and determination of Shunde's people.

As early as the late 1980s, some Shunde businesses already ventured abroad to set up overseas operations. Th move reflected the Shunde people's can-do spirit and courage. For instance, Leliu Huaxing Fan Factory and Rongqqi Dajin Clothing Factory set up factories in Cuba and New Zealand respectively.

The composition of Shunde's exports also changed dramatically in the 1980s. At the start of the 1980s, agricultural products and agricultural by-products were the main exports. By the end of the decade, industrial products like household electrical appliances had become the main exports. Electric fans, rice cookers, stationery, footwear, silk garments, cotton fabrics and other industrial goods were exported to more than 100 countries and regions like Japan, France, Germany, the United Kingdom, and the United States. This export composition transformation in the 1980s was speedier than what the 'Four Asian Tigers' (South Korea, Singapore, Taiwan and Hong Kong) experienced when they first started.

On the issue of the shortage of technical skills and professionals, Shunde launched several innovative talent policies:

(1) The government worked with TVEs to recruit outside talents through various channels. At the same time, it adopted a multiple-level, multiple-format and multiple-channel strategy to train local talents. By 1990, the number of competent talents (including teachers and doctors) rose to 15,260. The number was a 34.7-fold increase compared to 428 in 1982. Most of the talents worked in township enterprises. 2/3 of them came from other places of China, and the remaining 1/3 were trained locally.

(2) Giving up the traditional seniority and education qualification-based employment system, Shunde's businessmen adhered to the results-oriented market-based economy and adopted the principle of meritocracy on employment practices. According to the principle of meritocracy, Shunde gave many home-grown experts who had neither academic qualifications nor professional titles the positions and compensations that were consistent with their job performance.

(3) Most Shunde businesses implemented their own internal job classification system rather than job classification based on past academic qualifications or professional titles bestowed by the government. The change was a break from the then prevailing tradition where education attainments or professional titles determined one's job classification. The internal job classification system was merit-based, and the focus was on job performance. Freshly recruited technical personnel were first assigned to the factory floor. Based on their performance on the factory floor during the probation period, they were then assigned positions consistent with their ability and performance. Benefits accorded by the company were consistent with their positions and responsibilities. To reward outstanding employees, job appointments were not permanent, and they could quickly be promoted.

In 1991, Ma Jun, who had a PhD in Thermal Engineering from South China University of Technology, was employed by Midea. This move made the company the first TVE in the country to hire a PhD holder. Ma Jun's employment story became well-known in Shunde. In the summer of 1991, Ma Jun gave up a teaching job offer after he defended his PhD dissertation at the South China University of Technology. The move was unconventional at that time as a secured teaching job was the more popular career choice. Instead, he chose to market his research project, which was on energy-efficient air conditioners. After being rejected by several big companies, he was finally hired by He Xiangjian, General Manager of Midea, an electrical appliance TVE in Beijiao Town, Shunde. Although Midea was just a medium-sized TVE, He Xiangjian was a visionary. He broke the tradition of requiring fresh recruits to go through three months of probation and low starting wages when he hired Ma Jun. As a result, although Ma Jun started with a relatively small salary, he was exempted from the probation. In return, He Xiangjian asked Ma Jun to finish the energy-efficient aircon prototype in four months.

Three months later, Ma Jun successfully produced the first high-efficiency air conditioner prototype. Upon expert appraisal, it was determined that the output-to-weight ratio of the new air conditioner substantially exceeded the government-mandated standard, and its energy usage was 30% better as compared to air conditioners with the same weight. Midea immediately set up the production line to produce the new energy-saving air conditioners, with orders quickly exceeding 100 million yuan. Ma Jun was promoted to be a senior engineer and director of the factory, and his monthly salary increased several folds.

By the early 1990s, Shunde's economic development was in full swing. On average, the county-level city launched a new product every other day. A significant contributor to this burst of innovation was a conducive working environment for engineering and technical personnel. They were given sufficient funding and corresponding facilities for their research and were encouraged to establish an innovative culture. They were also represented in corporate decision making. Shunde's merit-based employment system was a crucial factor in the subsequent growth of many initially-small TVEs that later became giant corporations.

The evolution of Shunde's manufacturing industry

Shunde had a business development strategy from the beginning. TVEs engaged in compensation trade as they faced the problem of shortage of funds, skills and technology. By working for joint venture partners under the compensation trade, they acquired needed technology, capital goods, management expertise, and knowledge on the world market.

After acquiring the production skills, experience and export channels through the compensation trade, Shunde's manufacturers also possessed sufficient capital by then to form joint ventures with new overseas partners. In this change of business model, Shunde's manufacturers began partnering with others.

After 1987, the labour-intensive TVEs specialising in the compensation trade gradually decreased in Shunde, and local businesses either formed a joint venture with foreign partners under the umbrella of foreign-funded enterprises or started their own export operations. By the end of 1991, Shunde had set up 579 joint venture businesses. These businesses had an annual output value of 4.8 billion yuan and an export value of 320 million US dollars. At the same time, the processing fees of the compensation trade companies dropped to 1 million US dollars.

Although joint ventures were a gateway to the international market, there were certain limitations. They did not directly access the market, and foreign investors usually controlled the sourcing of production equipment and raw materials.

In terms of 'standing alone in the world market', Shunde entrepreneurs had two ways to achieve this. Firstly, after the contracts of their compensation trade businesses expired, their foreign-funded factories were turned over to local ownership. By leveraging on existing production technology, investment was increased to expand production, and new local brands were developed, thereby developing both their domestic and foreign markets. Secondly, advanced equipment was brought in to improve the production efficiency of the existing businesses and make new high-end products for the international market.

In the 1980s, Shunde imported more than 30,000 pieces of new production equipment with a total value of more than 300 million US dollars. The new equipment significantly boosted the competitiveness of Shunde's businesses internationally.

At the end of 1991, Shunde had 262 enterprises with annual sales exceeding 10 million yuan. Of these, 15 had sales between 50 million and 100 million yuan, and 21 had sales over 100 million yuan. Sixteen of these were TVEs. By then, the technology of these pillar enterprises had already reached the level which was achieved internationally in the late 1970s and early 1980s.

From an agricultural county short on funds, technology and production skills, Shunde became an important light industry manufacturing hub of the world in a decade. The phenomenal growth of Shunde's manufacturing industry looked more impressive than Taiwan and South Korea in the 1960s.

Economic restructuring in 1993

Many TVEs had severe management problems in the early 1990s. The direct consequence of the government's role as the owner of TVEs created a serious agency problem, and the government suffered from a 'limited benefit, unlimited liability' problem as more TVEs in the system suffered losses by the early 1990s. At that time, the non-performing loans (NPL) in Shunde's banking system exceeded 30%, mostly on loans to TVEs.

At the beginning of 1993, Shunde used the term 'glorious achievements amid frightening burdens' when reporting problems of its economic development. During that year, Shunde piloted China's first property rights reform. Many local state-owned TVEs were privatised, and the new property rights bestowed on management significantly boosted the productivity of the affected entities. As a result of the restructuring in 1993, many TVEs thrived. Many of Shunde's most prominent businesses today were a result of the reorganisation.

From 'coming in' to 'going out'

By forming partnerships with leading companies to invest in Chinese production or buying their technology through licensing or royalty payments, Shunde's businesses used the 'coming in' strategy to describe the process of adopting, modifying and then innovating on the imported production technology. This process is the recipe for success of Shunde's manufacturers, and many of them rank among the leading manufacturers in their industries today. They have developed their in-house technologies and possess considerable financial muscle to proceed with worldwide acquisitions of foreign companies or technology.

Through foreign investment and cooperation, Shunde's businesses used the 'going out' strategy to acquire technology, brands and markets for internationalisation. In recent years, many prominent Shunde businesses have been taking advantage of incentives offered in their existing export markets to relocate some of their operations overseas. This 'going out' strategy reinforced Shunde's manufacturers' overseas market positions. Shunde's industrial economy is export-oriented. At present, Shunde has trading relations with more than 200 countries and regions.

By the end of 2017, there were 133 cases of approved overseas investment. The total investment amount was about 6.285 billion US dollars. Twelve companies in Shunde set up 26 production bases overseas, with a total investment of 633.2 million US dollars. Among them, Midea's six production bases accounted for 507.9 million US dollars, and Keda's five production bases and one after-sales service centre accounted for 65 million US dollars. The remaining ten companies with 14 production bases invested a total of about 60 million US dollars. Investment regions were scattered in 15 countries in Southeast Asia, Africa and Europe.

Internationalisation of Midea's electrical appliances is a typical Shunde model. It can be divided into three stages. The first stage is to improve domestic production and make China the world's factory. The second stage is to establish an international distribution network and foreign production bases and to become shareholders of global brands. The last step is to finally become a brand owner.

At the start of the 21st century, Midea accelerated the setting up of its overseas sales network. Major branches were set up in Europe and New York, and sales offices were set up in Japan, Singapore, and South Korea.

Table 1. Overseas investment over the years

Year	Accumulated total as of 2010	2011	2012	2013	2014	2015	2016	2017
Investment amount (in million USD)	150	20	190	12	80	27	764	5040
Number of enterprises	27	9	7	6	14	14	21	22

In 2007, Midea's first overseas production base was completed and put into operation in Ho Chi Minh City, Vietnam. It had an annual production capacity of 5 million to 8 million small household appliances. At present, Midea has 21 factories and 260 logistic centres in more than 200 countries around the world. Overseas sales have exceeded 50% of its business.

In 2016, Midea launched a large-scale global expansion where it acquired 80.1% of Toshiba White Goods Division, a leading Japanese home appliances company. Midea also obtained the right to use the Toshiba brand name globally and more than 5,000 patents related to white appliances. In January 2017, 94.55% of the KUKA Group, the world's leading supplier of robotics and automation equipment, was acquired for 4.5 billion euros.

At present, Shunde's businesses' footprint has reached six continents. Shunde precision machinery manufacturer, Yizumi Precision Machinery Co., Ltd. has set up production bases in North America and India, and it is increasing its overseas business to 30% of sales. Global microwave manufacturing leader Galanz has sales and retail centres in the United States, Britain, France, Germany and other countries, and its export sales account for 60% of the company's business.

Shunde's businesses have also set up overseas R&D institutions to facilitate innovation and globalisation. They have developed innovative products and earned differentiated competitive advantages in the international market.

The leading Shunde company, Midea, has set up R&D facilities in the United States, Japan, Italy, Germany, and other countries. Among them, the Louisville Home Appliances R&D Centre in the United States was set up to take advantage of Louisville's home appliances research ecosystem. And the second one in Silicon Valley was set up to take advantage of the digital and high-tech talents there. By the end of 2017, the Louisville Home Appliances R&D Centre had submitted more than 45 patent applications in the United States, and the 6-month old Silicon Valley Future Technology Centre has successfully developed two AI-based smart home appliances and achieved many AI application breakthroughs in home appliances. Fang Hongbo, chairman of the Midea Group, has maintained that if the company wants to make new breakthroughs, resources should be deployed in leading research centres where Midea has no presence.

Shunde-based Yizumi has followed the same path of setting up an overseas R&D centre to acquire new technology. The company hired ENGEL's retired chief engineer and his team to set up an R&D institution in Europe. ENGEL is one of the world's largest injection moulding machine manufacturers. In 2017, the institute set up an R&D centre in Germany and became a member of the Aachen University of Plastics Processing Research Institute. The advanced robotic flexible manufacturing centre developed by Yizumi and the Aachen University of Plastics Processing Institute IKV is currently moving into the production phase.

Galanz has also established R&D institutions in many countries such as the United States, South Korea, Japan and the United Kingdom. In 2006, it set up the Galanz Korea R&D Centre in Seoul, South Korea. Other R&D centres soon followed. The company's international R&D experts are engaged in cutting-edge home appliances technology development such as smart appliances network development and using new materials in home appliances.

From a global R&D innovation perspective, Shunde's businesses in their 'going out' strategy have invested in overseas factories to gain market share, particularly in developing countries. They have also invested in R&D facilities in developed countries to tap into high-quality innovation resources like talents and technologies. By effectively absorbing technological spill-overs from developed countries, they have accelerated the upgrading of their manufacturing operations.

Shunde businesses going global

Going out to get new business partners and acquiring production capacity and technology, while at the same time attracting inward investment is the new strategy adopted by the now world-class Shunde manufacturers. The new strategy can be illustrated using two examples.

(1) By 'going out' to discuss cooperation with Hannover Exhibition Company, Shunde brought in the Hannover Robotics Academy as well as Guangdong (Tanzhou) International Exhibition Co. Ltd. to set up the Foshan Robotation Academy together. The goal of the institute is to train robotics specialists in China and promote the industry.

(2) In 2016, Midea Group acquired the majority stake of KUKA Group by 'going out', and it partnered KUKA in the 'coming in' stage to invest 10 billion yuan in the Shunde Sino-German Industrial Services Zone to set up the 80-hectare KUKA Smart Manufacturing Technology Park. The park houses four business segments: intelligent manufacturing, intelligent logistics, intelligent healthcare, and intelligent homes. Together, Midea and KUKA will market the products of the park in the world market.

The internationalisation of Shunde's enterprises will further integrate local enterprises into the world economy. The Guangdong-Hong Kong-Macau Greater Bay Area will promote the economic and technological development of the entire Pearl River Delta, and further enhance the globalisation of Shunde's businesses.

Chapter 8

Shunde's Innovations

Shunde is rich in natural resources and has experience in operating a cash-crop agricultural economy. By improving and perfecting the 'mulberry dyke and fish pond model' for hundreds of years, Shunde locals were knowledgeable about how the market economy ran and understood the importance of efficiency and sustainability in running businesses. In contrast to subsistence farmers, Shunde locals had extensive experience working as artisans, workers and merchants — the employment model that was a forerunner of work specialisation in the modern economy. The spirit of innovation and entrepreneurship was deeply ingrained in the culture of the Shunde populace, and this awareness flourished after 1978.

The mulberry dyke and fish pond model and today's recycling economy

The mulberry dyke and fish pond model was a system designed to maximise the potential of all production resources in the Pearl River Delta region. It was environmentally friendly and very efficient in resource utilisation. Production steps involved digging deep fish ponds, elevating the dyke surrounding the pond, planting mulberries along with the dyke bases, and farming freshwater fish in the pond.

The production cycle started from planting mulberry trees to engaging in silkworm farming and ended with selling the fish raised from feeding silkworm waste. An environmentally-friendly ecosystem with almost zero waste and where mulberry, silkworm and fish were created — the farmer planted mulberry trees along the dyke and used the leaves to feed the silkworms. Silkworm waste was fed to the fish, and after harvesting the fish, the fish waste that had accumulated at the bottom of the pond was excavated and used to strengthen the dyke base and served as fertiliser for the mulberry trees. In this system, both silk and fish were the final products. The process was a production chain, and what happened at one stage affected the other stages. It was, therefore, crucial to maintain efficiency at each stage and manage the entire system holistically. A famous saying in the Pearl River Delta summed up the relationship between organisms in the ecosystem: healthy mulberry trees lead to healthy silkworms, healthy fishes, good-quality fertiliser, and more silkworm cocoons. As the raw silk was an export commodity and its price subject to global market fluctuations, the Shunde populace developed an early knowledge of the worldwide economy and the operation of the market. Fish was a cash agricultural product and was sold to neighbouring cities. Hence the Shunde populace also learnt about being a cash agricultural product trader.

A complete, scientific and self-sustaining pond community, with the mulberry trees, silkworm, fish, and mud forming a symbiotic ecologically-friendly environment enhancing each other, was established. The system effectively prevented waterlogging of low areas as the pond was dredged after the fish harvest and the soil was used to build up the dyke and provide fertiliser to the mulberry trees along the embankment. All silkworm waste and fish waste were used again in the system, eliminating environmental pollution.

The 'mulberry fish pond' model was a forerunner of today's much-touted recycling and sustainable economy.

Development of the fish pond not only developed businesses related to the mulberry, silkworm and fish farming, it also drove silk-related manufacturing businesses.

In the heyday of the silk industry at the turn of the 20th century, Shunde was a famous town for Guangdong's economy. In 1922, its raw silk production accounted for 97% of the total Pearl River Delta production and 80% of the province's raw silk exports. However, during the Great Depression, both price and sales plummeted, and by 1938 raw silk sales were only one-fifth of 1922's. The downturn reduced the size of the mulberry fish ponds significantly, and other crops, mainly sugarcane, slowly replaced many mulberry trees.

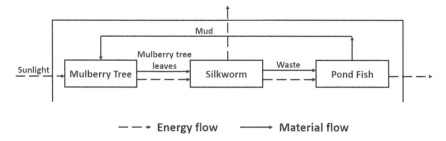

Figure 1. Mulberry fish pond model

The mulberry fish ponds remained a significant agricultural production model until the 1970s. The 1978 reform accelerated the decline of the silk industry. The sericulture required intense labour input and a long production cycle time, and carried higher risk, so most farmers gave it up and shifted to work at TVEs following industrialisation. The remaining mulberry fish ponds changed to fruit-based, flower-based, and sugarcane-based fish ponds. These crops required much less labour input, and by now, most mulberry fish ponds had disappeared in Shunde. After 1995, some ponds relocated to less developed peripheral areas of the Pearl River Delta. However, the emphasis on proper management and the orientation towards the market economy learnt from mulberry fish farming has become part of the entrepreneurial culture of the Shunde people.

Economic development model spearheaded by the Shunde government

Shunde has been an acknowledged leader in governance innovation since the Chinese reform started. The county built its economy around industrialisation in the early 1980s, and its commitment to the manufacturing industry has been steadfast. At different periods, the government pioneered innovative measures befitting the prevailing economic environment to promote economic growth. In the early days of reform, Shunde lacked funds, skills and technology. (For more information, please refer to 'Shunde and the World Economy'). The government controlled almost all of the meagre production resources, and its people had little resources of their own to

Figure 2. Mulberrydyke and fishpond

venture into productive endeavours. To jumpstart economic development, the government adopted the developmental state model, which was prevalent in East Asia. In this model, the governments of the four Asian Tiger economies played the 'innovative leader' role in galvanising the limited resources available and guiding the upgrade and transformation of the economy.

At the start of the reform, the initial conditions for industrialisation present in Shunde were poor. The central and provincial governments focused their industrial investment on Shunde's neighbouring provincial capital city, Guangzhou, which had an existing industrial base, while foreign investment from Hong Kong and Macau flocked to Shenzhen's Special Economic Zone due to favourable policies. As an agricultural-based county that was handicapped by a traditional socialist system that used the agricultural surplus to support industrialisation, the county could not generate enough excess capital for industrial investment. The Shunde government had to adopt innovative policies to solve this problem.

The government's innovative reform process

In the 1980s, the Shunde government adopted the developmental state model. This model emphasised manufacturing and collective ownership and encouraged hidden industry champions. In August 1978, the Shunde government allowed Rongqi Town and Hong Kong Dajing Co., Ltd to jointly set up the Rongqi Dajin Clothing Factory (Rongqi Town and Guizhou Town were merged in 2000 to form today's Ronggui Town). Dajin Clothing Factory was one of China's first TVEs to engage in the compensation trade export model. (For more information, please refer to 'Shunde and the World Economy.') The success of the model enabled Shunde to become the leading 'four tiger cubs of Guangdong'.

The 'four tiger cubs of Guangdong' refer to Nanhai, Shunde, Dongguan and Zhongshan. These four small and medium-sized counties in the Pearl River Delta were the pioneers in China's economic liberalisation in the 1980s.

The four counties' economies took off in the 1980s, and the 'tiger cub' nickname reflected their success and was comparable to the then-popular four Asian tigers of Hong Kong, Singapore, South Korea and Taiwan, although at a smaller scale. Each of the cubs had its economic model; Shunde, Zhongshan and Nanhai's models relied more on local entrepreneurs, while Dongguan's model relied more on overseas investment from Hong Kong, Macau and Taiwan. All the models were based on the manufacturing industry, and they had contributed to the making of the Pearl River Delta as the factory of the world in the 2000s. The four counties grew to become critical constituents of today's Guangdong-Hong Kong-Macau Greater Bay Area.

Under the compensation trade export model, the foreign partner provided funds, machinery, technology, management staff and raw materials, while the Shunde partner provided the factory floor and labour. The foreign partner bought all the finished products for export and paid the factory rental and the labour component of the product to the local partner after deducting the corresponding payment over the use of the equipment and other capital input they provided. The compensation trade model relieved most of the investment commitment from local Chinese partners sans labour and factory space and allowed them to build up their industries at a period when they could not raise enough funds to invest in industries.

The Chinese provision of labour input skillfully used the fact that labour at that time was extremely cheap — only about 10% of international standard and aplenty in China. In the case of land and factory space, the Chinese just converted old factories or constructed simple ones based on local materials. Again, not much investment was needed.

At the end of the contractual period in which the local Chinese partner had settled all obligations to their foreign partners over the use of their investment, the Chinese partners acquired all assets to become independent TVEs.

Many TVEs adopted the compensation model (please refer to 'The Shunde Economic Phenomenon' for more details), and Shunde resolved the problem over the shortage of funds, skills and production technology that existed during the earlier stage of reform. The local partners behind the TVEs were fast learners; they not only learnt the production skills used in the production of the first export products but also improved the process and earned the trust of overseas customers. At the end of the cooperation period, they not only retained their original export market but expanded it. The use of international export standards as a production benchmark also gave them a leg ahead of domestic Chinese competitors regarding quality. By the late 1980s, Shunde manufacturers had carried an implicit seal of quality among Chinese consumers, and TVEs had both the technical know-how and the management skills to expand in both the Chinese domestic market and overseas market. Many TVEs changed their business model from the compensationtrade to joint partner arrangements with foreign partners. The larger TVEs could already export on their own and operate freely without international partners.

The initial partners involved in the compensation trade mostly came from Hong Kong and Macau and focused on light industry. The 1980s' TVE business and operational model helped Shunde integrate into the world economy, and light industry remains a strong pillar of Shunde's economy today.

To facilitate the growth of TVEs and help them in their export drive, Shunde implemented a series of administrative reforms in the 1980s. The change devolved employee hiring power and wage policies to the factory manager — a departure from the socialist system that placed hiring power on bureaucrats and stressed the wage equality of workers. The factory manager could use a differentiated wage structure to pay his workers based on output and their contributions to the company, and he could hire and fire a worker without any interference from bureaucrats. While the abovementioned management prerogative of the factory manager was a standard operating procedure in the outside world at that time, the policy was a first in China.

The Chinese economy in the early 1980s was in an initial transition phase from a socialist economy to a market-based economy. A lot of government policies were based on trial-and-error, and the famous quotation 'crossing the river by touching the stones' was used to describe the policy environment. Some of the policies that came from the central government did not adequately address issues on the ground, and the Shunde government addressed this mismatch by slightly twisting the original directive from the central and provincial governments. It creatively retained the spirit and policy objective of the original guidelines while taking local conditions into account, thus making those policies workable in the local setting. During that period, the term 'transformer' was used to describe the Shunde government: the central and the provincial governments were power plants that send out high voltage output, and the local government acted as a transformer and lowered the input voltage to make it suitable for local consumers. This transformer description demonstrated the pragmatic spirit that Shunde's local government adopted in reforms, and the spirit of innovation was the secret recipe behind the success of the county over the past 40 years.

By being creative to pioneering in the compensation trade model and putting in place complementary policies to support its success, Shunde was the first to open the door to foreign investments in China. Shunde's reform and opening up was held in high esteem by the central government, and it was chosen by the government to pilot many new policies.

Property rights reform: targeting profitable rather than loss-making TVEs

In 1992, Shunde was selected to pilot the Guangdong province's comprehensive reform plan. Shunde seized this opportunity and became the first in China to implement a comprehensive reform which focused on TVE property rights. The drive converted not only money-losing TVEs to private ownership but also money-making ones.

Shunde was the first local government in China to implement the privatisation of collectively owned TVEs. The move generated some controversy at the beginning but proved to be highly successful. The property right reform, implemented in 1993, was named '靚女先嫁' in the local Cantonese dialect and it meant to marry off the family's beautiful daughter first. The same strategy was used in the 1993 property rights reform, and TVEs and local SOEs that had good management records and were profitable were the first to be included in the reform. This policy was controversial when first introduced because many believed that the change should target only the loss-making companies.

However, the policy proved successful, and Shunde's economy continued to move into high gear. Many economists attributed its success in the 1990s and 2000s to the removal of the agency problem in TVEs when they were privatised in 1993. After the privatisation of well-managed TVEs and local SOEs, management was incentivised to improve their business operations.

The success of the 1993 reform convinced many local governments in China to also adopt the policy.

The property rights reform laid the foundation for Shunde's current private-business-led economy. In 2017, private businesses accounted for nearly 80% of industrial output value and more than 90% of industrial output growth. The dominance of domestic private manufacturers in the local economy is a distinguishing feature of Shunde's industrial landscape.

Shunde was chosen to pilot the 1999 administrative modernisation reform

In 1999, Shunde was selected as the pilot county to experiment on administrative modernisation reform. It reoriented the government's policy objectives from that of a regulator to a service-centric type. The business-friendly environment helped the county become the top county in China for four consecutive years (2000 to 2003). It was also the first county whose GDP exceeded 100 billion yuan (2006).

In 2009, under the premise of maintaining the organisational structure, Shunde was allowed to manage the economic, social, cultural and other aspects of the prefecture-level city authority to carry out large-scale administrative reform.

Combining government functions to a smaller number of departments was a vital part of the 2009 administrative reform. By redefining government functions and aggregating similar tasks to fewer departments, administrative efficiency was improved.

Power over commerce, local taxation, food safety, land usage, urban planning, public security, social security management and many other areas were devolved from the provincial and municipal government to Shunde's district government. In most areas relating to economic development, Shunde's official ranking was elevated from a district under the Foshan city government to that of a county directly under the Guangdong provincial government.

In the reform, Shunde consolidated 41 party, government and grassroots-government-funded non-administrative organisations into 16 departments. These 16 departments included six administration departments, five economic departments, and five social service departments. This streamlining process led Shunde government to become the district government with the least number of departments in China. In November 2010, the government department streamlining experience was promoted to 25 other counties by the Guangdong provincial government.

Intensifying the innovation drive to build a high-tech Shunde

The competitive advantage which Shunde enjoyed in the past now faces challenges from newcomers who have imitated its model at a lower cost. Using economies of scale to lower costs; building an ecosystem and an efficient supply chain to offer innovative, cost-effective products; speeding up technological innovation and improving product design is now insufficient to sustain fast economic growth.

Moving into emerging high-value-added industries is the best option for Shunde's economic growth. However, this move is constrained by problems such as insufficient innovation capability, shortage of relevant talents and the fact that Shunde has little core technologies in emerging high-value-added industries. To address the shortcomings, the Shunde government has developed a technological development plan called 'Technology Shunde'. The programme is intended to work alongside the GBA project and develop Shunde's high-value-added emerging industries.

The Shunde government announced a series of measures aimed at promoting innovation. The focus was on seven aspects: nurture high-tech enterprises, build new R&D institutions, improve enterprise technology, build incubators, develop core technologies in the targeted industries, build up an innovative talent pool, and promote fintech.

In March 2016, the Shunde government established a Financial Development Bureau to promote fintech, support promising new high-tech start-ups and help emerging industries obtain finance for expansion. Kecan Group, a venture capital holding company, was set up by the Shunde government to invest in technology park construction and establish incubators to attract talents. Kecan also set up incubators in Shenzhen with the aim of convincing successful start-ups at the Shenzhen incubator to move to Shunde once their products have reached the commercial production phase. Similarly, Kecan set up an office in Beijing to attract successful start-ups to move to Shunde for their manufacturing operations. A one-billion-yuan venture capital fund was set up by Kecan to invest in promising start-ups in Shunde.

Shunde has 14 innovation platforms under operation, and they can be classified into three groups. The first group comprises six platforms related to servicing home appliances, furniture, horticulture, and the garment and machinery industries. They provide business consultancy, testing, design and training services to the industries.

The second group comprises five platforms in fundamental research related to the industries. The district government has cooperated with universities and research institutes to set them up, and they provide postgraduate research training, conduct application-type research and focus on adapting the research findings into production.

The last group comprises three incubator platforms for innovative and entrepreneurial start-ups. Their businesses focus on forming teams, project incubation, and technology-based coaching for the enterprises.

On top of the 14 platforms, Shunde has also been building three important scientific and technological innovation clusters: the Sino-German Industrial Services Zone, the Wisdom Valley of Southern China, and the Shunde New High-Tech Industrial Development Zone. These clusters are found in the south, east and southwest regions of Shunde respectively.

The Sino-German Industrial Services Zone is an intelligent manufacturing industrial park; it focuses on smart manufacturing, robotics, and modern exhibitions. The Wisdom Valley of Southern China is an area designed to attract company headquarters, talents, as well as high-end R&D and service industries. The High-Tech Zone comes with complete facilities and impressive ecological design and serves as a modern industrial base for businesses.

Promoting high-value-added emerging industries is on the to-do-list for most GBA second-tier cities, and attractive financial incentives are offered to attract successful companies to locate to their towns. For Shunde, the government believes that aside from financial incentives, other non-economic factors like providing conducive business and living environments are what attracts talents and emerging industries. Some reforms have recently been implemented to facilitate business operations and help outside talents relocate to Shunde. An example is the 1121 Reform, which aims to create a conducive business environment by streamlining business procedures and providing quality support services.

Shunde is known for implementing comprehensive plans to attract talents and industries. The skill reflects Shunde's creative spirit and its ability to think out of the box, and is the hidden factor contributing to its success.

Innovative management of private companies

The rise of Shunde's home appliances industry reflects the entrepreneurial spirit and innovative ability of its private companies. Entrepreneurs in the home appliances industry understand the company's strengths and weaknesses, and their business model leverages on internal strength and avoids pitfalls related to its shortcomings. They buid large industry supply chains, achieve economies of scale, and speedily incorporate the latest product design and technology innovation in their products. Shunde's home appliances are known for being cost-effectiveness. But, most of the innovations in Shunde's home appliances industry are applied ones, few of them touch basic functions.

Shunde went through three industry evaluations in the past 12 years and is undisputedly the country's home appliances capital. Since China's reform and opening, the industry has attracted more than 3,200 home appliances and complementary companies using imitation, import and innovation.

It currently has an output value of over 200 billion yuan. There are 84 home appliances companies with sales of over 100 million yuan, and 4 with sales of over 10 billion yuan. These four companies include Midea, Hisense, Galanz and Vanward. Additionally, 200 companies are among China's top 500 corporations. In recent years, new emerging stars such as Viomi and Deerma have surfaced, and GMCC and Sunwill have become invisible industry champions.

Shunde's home appliances industry currently has five national-level technology centres and 21 provincial-level technology centres. It has the highest number of national-level technology centres in the country and holds one of the highest numbers of patents. By 2017, the industry includes more than 200 national high-tech companies.

Another feature of Shunde's home appliances industry is that many companies are willing to work in a niche area. Apart from large companies like Midea, many companies sell a single range of products but have an output value of 500 million to 1 billion yuan. The extent of specialisation in the home appliances industry of Shunde is uncommon in China.

Branding also plays an indispensable role in Shunde's home appliances companies. After being named China's home appliances capital again in 2014, Shunde further implemented a movement to market its brand regionally and internationally. There is no surprise that in 2018, Shunde was once again crowned the home appliances capital. It has nine home appliances brand classified as nationally famous brands, almost one-third of famous national brands, 31 famous provincial brands and 57 well-known provincial brands.

Shunde's trademark registration data fully reflects the emphasis on brand innovation. Currently, the number of famous brands in the region, famous brands in Guangdong province, collective trademarks, and international trademark applications in Madrid are 34, 143, 21 and 229 respectively. More than 93,000 valid registered trademarks have been filed, and the district boasted an average business trademark of 4,800 per ten thousand business entities, among the highest in China.

The challenge of continuing innovation

However, Shunde's home appliances also face the problem of continuing innovation challenges. Most of its innovations are application innovations rather than entirely new product innovations or essential function innovation. The industry is moving to address this issue by doing more basic research, acquiring technology from overseas and moving into complementary technology to search for a breakthrough.

In the context of fierce international competition brought by the new industrial revolution and the challenges posed by other cities in GBA following the closer integration of Pearl River Delta economy, Shunde's government will face new opportunities and challenges when trying to guide private companies innovatively. Competitors from all around the world and the GBA will be fighting for the same talents and companies, making the goal to build a high-tech Shunde a more difficult one. Regarding opportunities, however, cooperation in the GBA may be beneficial for Shunde's industries as Shunde can tap into the vast talent pool and business opportunities offered by Shenzhen and Guangdong. A case in point is the relocation of DJI's manufacturing facility into Shunde. DJI is the largest civilian drone manufacturer in the world, and it has chosen Shunde for its expansion.

The GBA integration presents both a challenge and an opportunity to Shunde; as long as Shunde's government and private companies continue to innovate, the GBA will become an essential platform for Shunde's economic development.

Chapter 9

Shunde's Successful Reforms

Shunde's economic success is marked by a series of reforms led by generations of passionate and enterprising Shunde people. Shunde pioneered many far-reaching reforms in China, and the district (county, city) was chosen multiple times as the national or provincial reform pilot area. Since China's reform and opening up, Shunde has experienced at least one major reform in every decade. Each reform accelerated the district's economic and social development, and it can be argued that reforms are the source of Shunde's success.

History of reforms in Shunde

In the 1970s, the Shunde county government announced an economic development policy of building agriculture-based industries and using agricultural industrialisation to generate a surplus that will promote further industrialisation. As a result, several agricultural-based industrial enterprises were set up. Shunde set up one of the country's first compensation trade TVEs — Dajin Clothing Factory, and its success prompted the setting up of other TVEs that engaged in the same trading model. Shunde became the pioneer in export compensation trade model, and almost all its villages had their TVEs.

In the 1980s, Shunde's government promulgated a three-way development strategy: develop an industrialisation-led economic growth model, focus on collective ownership, and promote industry champions as a pillar of growth. The three-way model was so successful that it facilitated Shunde's transformation from an agriculture-based economy to an industry-based economy and enabled Shunde to become the most prosperous county in Guangdong. As a result, Shunde became the leading 'Guangdong four tiger cubs' economy (the other fast-growing cubs were Nanhai, Dongguan and Zhongshan).

Shunde's economy took off in the 1990s. In 1991, its government revenue was the highest amongst all counties in China. In 1992, its total industrial output was 49.5% higher than the year before, an extremely rare feat in the world's industrial development history. However, the economic success also brought along an agency problem and debt crisis. By 1992, Shunde had 259 TVEs with serious financial problems, 109 of which were close to insolvency. To solve these problems, the Shunde government put forward the idea of property rights reform.

In 1992, Shunde was assigned to be Guangdong's comprehensive reform pilot county, and a series of sweeping reforms focusing on property rights was introduced. Complementary administrative reforms in areas such as streamlining bureaucracy, simplifying administrative procedures, and establishing a business-friendly government structure that emphasised the development of the socialist market economic system, were implemented to support the property rights reform. The property rights reform started by privatising state-owned enterprises (SOEs) that had fewer problems to avoid the impression that the government's reform objective was to jettison money-losing businesses while keeping money-making ones. Some of the most successful local private businesses today, such as Midea Group and Galanz Group, traced their origin to the 1992 property rights reform.

In 1999, Shunde was the first pilot city in China to experiment on means to become a modern city.

In 2009, Shunde implemented a large-scale administrative reform to streamline government operations further. 41 party and government organisations were consolidated into 16 departments.

In 2018, Shunde was chosen as a 'high-quality administrative development and innovative reform experimental zone'. The idea behind the appointment was to replicate successful economic and social reforms that attract and nurture advanced manufacturing industries to other localities in Guangdong province, and the focuses are on city administration and planning, land use, construction management, and a policy framework that nurtures the new high-tech manufacturing industry. International benchmarks would be used to ensure that the development model and policy framework adopted the best practices available.

The purpose of reforms is to achieve improvement and breakthroughs. Although the reform process will be met with many obstacles and there is no guarantee of success, history has shown that Shunde's grit and willingness to tackle adversaries will enable it to rise above challenges and outperform itself.

The spirit behind Shunde's reforms

The Chinese government usually tests out reforms in pilot cities before pushing successful ones nationwide. Shunde is one of the said principal pilot cities chosen by both the national and provincial government. Although Shunde has been successful in piloting many reforms and many cities followed its footsteps to implement similar changes, on the ground, not many were able to replicate the results successfully. This divergence of results is attributable to the difference in attitude and mindset behind implementing the reforms, which affects how they are carried out. To find out more about how Shunde's traditional culture influenced reforms implementation, please read 'Shunde's Lingnan Culture'.

Shunde earned its role as a pivotal reform pilot centre through the ingenuity of its people. Unlike special economic zones, Shunde did not have many resources. However, it managed to transform from an agricultural-based county in the Pearl River Delta to an important manufacturing city in the Greater Bay Area. Its success can be attributable to several factors:

1. Shunde's traditional value emphasises humility, hard work, and pragmatism. The reform and opening up provided the perfect platform for this spirit to be showcased and its people aptly used this opportunity.

Table 1. A partial list of awards won by Shunde

Event	Year
Rongqi Dajin Clothing Factory was the first enterprise in the country to adopt the compensation trade export model	1978
Held the first large-scale dragon boat competition	1980
Mulberry dyke fish pond artificial ecosystem was the first Chinese research project to be incorporated as a United Nations scientific research project	1981
Became the country's largest production centre for electric fans and was the county with the highest GDP in the province	1985
Produced China's first non-stick rice cooker	1988
Top county in China in export earnings	1990
Top county in China in government revenue	1991
Pioneer in property rights reform	1993
Top county in road density and road mileage	1995
Men and women dragon boat teams won 7 gold awards in the first World Dragon Boat Championship	1995
Production and sales of Galanz Group's microwave oven ranked first in the world	1998
Junan, Daliang and Rongqi were the first townships in China to hold the title 'Home of Chinese Performing Arts'	1999
Awarded the title 'Home of the Chinese Chefs'	2004
China's first mega furniture retail market built in Lecong Town	2004
Awarded the title 'Home of Chinese Dragon Boat'	2005
Shunde was awarded the title 'China's Home Appliances Capital', while Beijiao Town was awarded the title 'China's Home Appliances Manufacturing Town'	2006
Given the title 'Home of Chinese Eels'	2009
First pilot city to implement business administrative reforms	2012
Midea Group became the largest listed home appliances company in China	2013
Fengjian Village in Xingtan Town won the 2013 'Most Beautiful Village in China' award	2013
Won the 'Top 10 Prosperous District' title for ten consecutive years	2018
Won the 'Top District in China's Top 100 Districts' award for seven consecutive years	2012–2018

Shunde understood the rationale behind the country's reforms and developed policies that leveraged on the county's resource base. In the 1980s, it used cheap labour that resulted from farmers being displaced during rural industrialisation and used the export compensation trade model to accumulate capital and build expertise in light industries. In the 1990s, it used its accumulated capital and human resources to build world-class manufacturing plants, and in the 2000s, it moved upscale into higher value-added manufacturing industries. The ability to grasp the central government's reform spirit and to fit it into the local context is the key factor behind Shunde's successful implementation of the 'active government' concept. The reforms implemented by Shunde are not just a result of policies of the central government but are also a response to local development needs.

2. The Shunde government took on a leadership role in reforms. It cleverly handled the relationship between the government and the market by protecting property rights, respecting market discipline, and promoting market-friendly policies. When the economy slowed down due to bottleneck, the Shunde government faced the problems squarely and pushed for reforms that overcame the bottlenecks. When the central government restructured the country's machinery industry in 1979, Shunde's nascent primitive agricultural machinery sector shifted to light industrial sectors like garment industry, and Shunde moved into export markets. In 1993, the property rights reform was a drastic measure implemented when the county faced the debt crisis as a result of agency issue within TVEs. In 2009, the comprehensive reform was an attempt at improving government efficiency and building a service-oriented government right after Shunde became the first county in China to have achieved more than 100 billion in GDP, and the 2018 reform was introduced when China was entering a new norm, and Shunde needed to move into high value-added manufacturing.

3. Shunde's key to successful reform had a capable policy implementation team. Shunde emphasised the importance of having competent and enlightened leadership since the 1978 reform. It invested time and effort to nurture three specific teams at an early stage: these teams — the party cadres, entrepreneurs, and grassroots committees — executed reforms on the ground. The party cadre translated central and provincial government policies into local policies and executed them. It localised the reform's spirit and made local-friendly policies that increased the chance of the policies' success. The entrepreneur group had the business experience and means to speedily try out reform measures put forward by the

cadre group, and since there is a strong belief that the economy drives social development, most of the reforms, which are economic, garnered the support of private entrepreneurs. The entrepreneurs' understanding of the market proved to be invaluable, and they provided useful input regarding policy formulation. The grassroots committee was also a critical success factor behind Shunde's reforms. Even at an early stage, Shunde realised that economic reforms always carried a social implication. Since most of the complementary measures supporting the reforms were social, an active grassroots organisation was critical to ensure the effective implementation of the reform.

Shunde always uses its accumulated economic resources to launch social reforms (for more information, please refer to 'Shunde's City Governance'), build a safe and stable living environment and instil a sense of confidence in government reforms. The society understands that reforms are only a means to achieve social development, and its unwavering support for development strategies provide a reliable safety net for the continuity of both economic and social reforms. The consistency in believing in the reforms is remarkable in Shunde. Shunde has always adhered to a manufacturing-led economic growth model that prioritises manufacturing. It has also subscribed to a liveable city development model which emphasises on the economic aspects of social reform. Thanks to this longstanding coherence between strategic belief and policy support, Shunde has developed rapidly.

Future reforms in Shunde

1. Focus on the 'create two spaces, promote three directions, build five themes' strategy. This comprehensive strategy was introduced by Shunde in 2018. 'Create two spaces' refers to creating a physical and regulatory space for businesses to exercise their creativity and grow their business. The goal is to build a society where it is easy to start and grow a business and provide an environment that includes transparency and best practices. 'Promote three directions' refers to promoting smart manufacturing, innovative globalisation and green development to lead industries towards mid- to high-value. 'Build five themes' refers to building the

new Shunde along five themes: to be high-tech, cultural, beautiful, harmonious, and prosperous.

The reform focuses on implementing seven major tasks: strengthening innovation drive to build a high-tech Shunde, adhering to plans to ensure that urban construction leads to modernisation, remodelling village-level industrial parks and using the transformation to revitalise and develop villages, preserving culture to build a active and modern cultural zone, adhering to green development plans to build a beautiful Shunde, establishing a healthy and pervasive grassroots governance culture to build a harmonious Shunde, and assembling a disciplined administration team.

2. Successfully transform village-level industrial parks and create a space for high-quality development. Village-level industrial parks are a double-edged sword. On the one hand, they are the main obstacle impeding Shunde's growth and the source of safety production and environmental pollution problems. On the other hand, they provide the potential and opportunity for Shunde's future development. In 2018, the upgrading of village-level industrial parks became the top priority for the Shunde government, and on April 2018, the Shunde government convened a town hall meeting to announce the transformation of village-level industrial parks. Shunde created a 'government-led, market-oriented' redevelopment model which aims to build new green and modern industrial zones from decrepit old areas.

To transform village-level industrial parks, Shunde must phase out obsolete and polluting production facilities and promulgate measures to encourage innovative small- and medium-sized enterprises who can create high value-added business models to stay in the new industrial park. The government should proactively assist businesses and encourage high-end talents to relocate and work at Shunde. It must help promising local enterprises to raise capital and meet expansion requirements and attract investments that can serve as pillars in the industrial value chain. The new industrial park rejuvenation programme offers a host of opportunities to transform Shunde's economy.

3. Take the lead in building Guangdong province's high-quality administrative development and innovative reform experimental zone.

On September 19, 2018, Shunde was approved by Guangdong province to build a reform and innovation experimental zone for high-quality development. The primary purpose of the zone is to promote replicable reforms that will help provincial development. Shunde was given the administrative power to try out solutions that can solve legacy problems caused by its past, unregulated speedy growth, and also chart the path towards a greener, more sustainable and more equitable growth. The provincial government's encouragement to establish a 'Shunde model' that can be adopted by other localities in Guangdong is an acid test for Shunde, as well as a vote of confidence on its ability to think out of the box and make meaningful reforms. Guangdong province requested that Shunde focus its economic development based on advanced manufacturing, and accelerate the transformation of government functions and institutional innovation. Shunde is to explore areas like land use, spatial planning and construction to further optimise an innovative and business-friendly environment, to accelerate the formation of an institutional and administrative framework that promotes a modern and high-quality economy. The provincial government requested Shunde to benchmark its achievement against international best practices.

Taking the lead to become Guangdong province's high-quality reform and innovation experimental zone is an opportunity. To this reform, Shunde aims to again use market forces as a key driving force, ensure that it complements the GBA strategy, focus on transforming village-level industrial parks, and focus on high-quality development of the manufacturing industry.

Conclusion

Shunde's reform and development efforts will move full speed ahead. The cultural spirit behind the reforms has been a strong driving force towards Shunde's development, and this element will continue to support future reforms and promote Shunde as an important player in the GBA.

Shunde has built a tested policy implementation team that is highly capable of pushing innovative policies, a robust private entrepreneur team that is market savvy and has extensive experience both at home and overseas, and a grassroots leadership team with high public approval. These three pillars, together with favourable intrinsic motivations towards reforms, will lay a good foundation for the future development of Shunde.

The creation of a fair and efficient business environment, as well as a conducive and liveable environment for high-end migrant talents, are the key to attracting companies and talents. Shunde's accumulated knowledge and experience on reforms will make it indispensable in the GBA.

Chapter 10

Shunde's Emerging Industries

The new industrial revolution brings both opportunities and challenges to Shunde. On the one hand, opportunities allow Shunde to adopt new disruptive technologies to maintain leadership in key manufacturing sectors and to leapfrog its competitors. On the other hand, it faces challenges from competitors who might use the new technologies creatively to beat Shunde manufacturers.

Shunde's district government gives priority to several emerging industries. Among them are smart manufacturing and robotics, industrial design, tourism, modern conventions and exhibitions, and e-commerce. These industries are related to Shunde's current industrial base and can be considered as extensions of the existing industrial value chains. Working on industry extensions rather than creating new ones not only lowers the inherent risk of building new industries, it also cuts the learning curve and improves the chances of success. Shunde's smart decision has been beneficial to the initial development of these emerging industries.

Smart manufacturing and robotics

Developing the smart manufacturing and robotics industry is the driver in Shunde's industrial upgrading. It is the key to building a high-tech Shunde.

There are currently more than 80 companies in Shunde's robotics and smart manufacturing industry. Five of them (Jaten, Lixunda, Longsheng, Sanhe and Yaskawa Miyuki) have annual sales of more than 100 million yuan. They work in the mid-stream robot manufacturing and the downstream system integration part of the robotics industry value chain. Top robotic companies like Germany's KUKA and China's Efort have set up operations in Shunde, and emerging local companies like E-Deodar, Tiantai and Longsheng have developed their in-house robots for specialised operations. Most Shunde robotics companies work on the downstream system integration part of the industry — they adopt robots purchased from mid-stream robot manufacturers for the end-users' factory operations.

Among the five companies with output value exceeding 100 million yuan, Jaten's primary business is the manufacturing of the automatic guided vehicles (AGVs) used in smart warehouses, while Lixunda's is on manufacturing polishing robots for the home appliances industry. Sanhe's primary market is also in AGVs. It buys critical components such as servo-motors, speed reducers, and controllers from upstream component suppliers, and assembles the parts and add features specially tailored for the local market.

Longsheng and Yaskawa Miyuki are partners of Kawasaki and Yaskawa. They buy their partners' robots and modify them to fit local customer requirements.

Regarding their position in the industrial value chain, Jaten, Lixunda and Sanhe are mid-stream robot manufacturers while Longsheng and Yaskawa Miyuki are downstream system integrators. Of the five, Sanhe is the only one which has the reducer production capability. Shunde's robotics industry has few upstream precision parts manufacturers.

Smart manufacturing and robotics are usually considered a single industry and most of the significant players have them as separate divisions in the company. The ability to integrate robots in an automated production line is a critical competitive advantage for any major industry player. Shunde is banking on some of its foremost manufacturers to innovate, to accumulate experiences in smart manufacturing and robotics. The latest air-con manufacturing plant owned by Midea (built with KUKA's technical input) is known as one of the most advanced factories in China. Galanz Group has constructed a fully automated washing machine and microwave oven production line, and China's first smart water basin production facility, for Sakura Kitchen, is developed by ABB and Lixunda.

In recent years, the district government has launched a series of measures to promote the development of the smart manufacturing and robotics industry.

1. A robotics industry development fund is established to support companies in substituting humans with robots.
2. The government encourages the setting up of smart manufacturing industry clusters such as the Guangdong Province Smart Manufacturing and Innovation Park in Beijiao. Phase 1 of the park will focus on attracting mid-stream robot manufacturers as well as upstream component manufacturers in control systems, servomotors and high precision speed reducers. Phase 2 will house robotic start-up incubators, shared laboratories and R&D facilities.
3. Industrial upgrading is accelerated through cross-border cooperation and M&As. The most classic case is the joint venture between Midea and Yaskawa, which formed the Midea Yaskawa Service Robot Company as well as the Yaskawa Midea Industrial Robot Company. Midea also acquired KUKA and formed a joint venture with it to invest in Shunde's robotics industry. Midea also acquired the Israeli intelligent control software company Servotronix.
4. Local industry platforms are built to strengthen the robotics industry. The district government set up the Hannover Foshan Robotation Academy, South China Intelligent Robot Innovation Institution, National Industrial Robot Quality Supervision and Inspection (Guangdong) Centre, and Guangdong Intelligent Manufacturing Industry Demonstration Base. The joint Midea and KUKA intelligent manufacturing base are currently under construction, and the project includes a robot manufacturing centre, research centre and training centre.
5. Shunde government has sent investment missions to Germany to entice German robotics companies to set up operations in Shunde. Likewise, it has sent teams to domestic regions that are advanced in robotics (for instance, Beijing, Shanghai and Shenzhen) to promote the relocation of their firms to Shunde. Shunde government promises to provide special tailor-made incentives to attract qualified robotics and smart manufacturing companies.

Smart manufacturing and robotics involve many different disciplines and are very complex production processes. The multidisciplinary and high-tech nature of the industry requires a robust and comprehensive industrial supporting base. China is a late-comer to the industry as it went into robotics and automation only 10–15 years ago, while other advanced manufacturing economies had gone into robotics and factory automation in the 1980s. Therefore, China's industrial position in robotics and smart manufacturing businesses remains relatively weak.

In the robotics industry, upstream core components make up more than 70% of a robot's cost. At present, most of the local Chinese robotic companies operate in either the middle or downstream ends of robot assembly and systems integration. Weaknesses in the Chinese robotics industry include importing most of the core components, inadequate core technology, and products at the low- to mid-end of the market. More work needs to be done to upgrade Shunde's smart manufacturing and robotics industry. (For more information, please refer to 'Shunde's Industrial Parks'.)

Industrial design

In 2008, the National Intellectual Property Office approved the construction of a National Industry Design and Creative Industry Base in Shunde. The move marked the start of Shunde's industrial design industry. The district government was quick to promote the establishment of three major industrial design clusters: Guangdong Industrial Design City at Shunde, Shunde Creative Industry Park, and SKG Silicon Valley Incubation Park. These clusters successfully meet the industrial design requirement of Shunde's substantial industrial base.

The three parks progressively became national-level incubators and currently have nearly 40 high-tech design companies. Shunde is now Guangdong province's largest high-end, professional and international industrial design zone, attracting almost 10,000 designers from mainland China and overseas. Design institutes from Tsinghua University and Hong Kong Creative Design Centre have also set up offices in Shunde. The annual number of design patent applications has exceeded a thousand, and the yearly industrial output using industrial design produced at Shunde has run into tens of billions of yuan. Guangdong Industrial Design City is particularly outstanding; in 2018, it was awarded five stars for its high development quality. It is the only demonstration base in Guangdong province that has been awarded five stars, and it is the pillar of Shunde's industrial design industry.

Guangdong Industrial Design City officially opened in 2009. It currently houses 30 high-tech industrial design companies, three of China's top ten industrial design companies, three of Guangdong's industrial design centres, and 8,195 technological R&D staff. It has developed more than 20 local brands and introduced more than 6,000 new products to the market. It has also produced 3,191 patents. The successful conversion rate of the industrial park's output is particularly impressive — 85% of its designs have been put into production and turned into marketable products. The park had generated an accumulated revenue of nearly 3 billion yuan from 2009 to 2017. In 2017, it won 21 domestic and international design awards.

It also provides marketing research, industrial design, prototype development and manufacturing incubators, R&D, exhibitions and conventions, training, and many other services for the manufacturing industries in Shunde. Recently, it has expanded its service to support smart manufacturing, smart home, healthcare and other emerging industries.

It also houses the Guangdong Shunde Innovation Design and Research Institute which pairs graduate students and application-oriented research projects, providing talent support for local high-tech companies. As of June 2018, the research institute has 127 teaching staff with 118 of them working full-time. In 2017, it partnered with more than 50 Chinese universities to train 413 graduate students, carried out 21 research incubations projects and applied for 108 patents. The Institute has agreements with 69 local colleges and universities to teach graduate students in industrial design. It is the only education institution in China accredited by the government in this area.

Design City has gained a reputation both at home and abroad. In the first half of 2018, it received 234 groups of visitors with more than 5,000 people.

Shunde used its strong industrial design capability to come up with an innovative 'technology–design–industry' development concept. In recent years, the district government launched the 'Design Shunde' policy to support its manufacturing industry to move upscale using industrial design.

The 'Design Shunde Three-Year Action Plan (2018–2020)' was announced in September 2018 by the Shunde government. It involves spending 1.5 billion yuan to implement six projects and establish Shunde as a world-class industrial design centre.

The first project will double the space in Guangdong Industrial Design City to 200,000 square metres in three years and establish the design city as a vital component of the Belt and Road Initiative and the Greater Bay Area.

The second project aims to enhance the creative capability of the Design City and set up advanced industrial design research institutes there.

The third project aims to launch an industrial pairing project to link 1,000 traditional manufacturing companies with creative industrial design firms. The linkage is designed to help traditional manufacturing firms move up the value chain.

The fourth project relates to introducing favourable policies to attract talented industrial designers to work and live in Shunde.

The fifth project aims to set up a platform to attract overseas high-tech industrial design companies to set up offices in Shunde and to attract more international industrial design events to be held at Shunde.

The last project aims to create a good design industry ecosystem by providing a holistic living environment for design talents, a pleasant business environment in intellectual property rights, high technology integration with design, minimal regulation, and so on.

Tourism and modern exhibitions & conventions

In recent years, Shunde's water town and culinary culture tourism has developed rapidly. Tourism has become a significant driving force for the economic transformation of Shunde. In 2017, tourism revenue in the region was 15.53 billion yuan, a year-on-year increase of 8.3%. The hotel accommodation industry recorded revenue of 1.448 billion yuan, a year-on-year increase of 12.6%. The number of overnight visitors increased by 20.03% to 5.35 million, and visitors to A-rated scenic spots increased by 6.24% to 11.44 million.

Shunde has several A-rated tourism spots. Changlu Tourism Leisure Park is a national 5A tourist scenic spot. Qinghui Garden, Chencun Flower World, Louvre International Home Expo Centre, Lecong International Convention and Exhibition Centre, and Snoopy World are national 4A scenic spots. Fengjian Water Town, Chow Tai Fook Jewellery Cultural Centre, Bijiang Golden House and South China Silk Museum are national 3A scenic spots. There are also many unrated spots such as Shunde Museum as well as Bruce Lee Park, which is popular with tourist.

Shunde actively leverages on its manufacturing success as a unique tourist attraction. In Guangdong Industrial Design City, tourist attractions such as leisure parks for designers, industrial design exhibition halls as well as dining facilities have been added, and the result has been promising. The Louvre International Home Expo Centre skilfully combines elements in home interior design, furniture, Shunde food culture and first-class hotel accommodation and attracts more than 2 million tourists every year. Chow Tai Fook Jewellery Cultural Centre uses a jewellery culture showcase concept to integrate jewellery processing and tourism, providing tourists with a unique cultural and shopping experience.

The traditional dragon boat race, water town tour and culinary tour have all proven successful in attracting tourists. In particular, the annual Food Festival consistently draws in tourists. Since 2006, the annual Food Festival has been held in succession for 13 years, and activities include food exhibitions, cooking competitions, food and beverage R&D demonstrations, and so on.

International conventions and exhibitions are also promoted to integrate tourism and industry. Following the opening of Tanzhou International Convention and Exhibition Centre, the government has been supporting the Meeting Incentive Convention Exhibition (MICE) businesses for the joint development of high-end industries and tourism.

Tanzhou International Convention and Exhibition Centre is the core of developing the MICE industry. The centre occupies 300,000 square metres and has a total planned floor area of 400,000 square metres. The project comprises exhibition, conference and other facilities, and is Foshan's largest and most modern professional exhibition complex. The maximum floor loading weight is 10 tonnes, the highest among all exhibition centres in China, and allows almost all industrial exhibitions to be held in Shunde.

Phase one of the Tanzhou Centre has 50,000 square metres of exhibition space, and phase two involves doubling the show area to 100,000 square metres. The Centre can meet the diverse exhibition needs of different industries and will be the permanent exhibition centre for The Pearl River West Coast Advanced Equipment Manufacturing Exhibition, and the China Equipment Manufacturing Exhibition.

The Centre took in German exhibition giant Hannover Messe as a partner for the project. The German element, which is of high international standard, is apparent in the design, construction and operation of facilities. At present, China (Guangdong) 'Internet +' Expo and Pearl River West Coast Advanced Manufacturing Investment Exhibition are held there annually. Large-scale exhibitions for home appliances, furniture, and others are being launched, and some international exhibitions hosted by Hannover Messe are in the process of opening its Asia show at Tanzhou.

E-commerce

In addition to consumer goods manufacturing, Shunde is also a well-known home appliances centre in China. Shunde business people capitalise on this reputation and use it to build the emerging e-commerce industry. Shunde is designated as Guangdong's first e-commerce innovation zone. The Shunde government continually innovates and promotes e-commerce by implementing supporting policies, fostering the development of an e-commerce ecosystem and building e-commerce parks to draw in key businesses and platforms.

There are more than 15 e-commerce platforms at Shunde, and the number of online merchants engaged in B2B and B2C transaction has exceeded 10,000. The district has 20 e-commerce parks, each with a distinct focus, in operation or under construction. Among them is Longjiang Furniture Industrial Park which is recognised by the Ministry of Commerce as the country's e-commerce demonstration base.

Shunde is home to 25 of Guangdong province's top 100 e-commerce companies, second to Shenzhen, the well-known innovation centre. It has 118 e-commerce companies that are considered leaders in their respective fields.

According to statistics, Shunde's e-commerce transaction volume reached 234.017 billion yuan in 2017. During the 2018 Singles' Day shopping festival, Shunde e-commerce clocked in a 9.2-billion-yuan turnover on just that day, a year-on-year increase of 20%. Companies that recorded more than 100 million yuan of sales on that day included Midea, Merid, Pingo International, China Macro and many more. Many companies also became champions in their industry category; for instance, Pingo International in the home furniture section and Midea in the small household appliances section.

Home appliances e-commerce has always dominated Shunde's e-commerce industry. In recent years, however, e-commerce has diversified and included house paint, food, furniture and other areas. The industry is rapidly expanding, and large companies like Midea, Galanz and Pingo International are shifting their marketing efforts online.

Leveraging the strength of its manufacturing industry, Shunde has chosen to focus on developing e-commerce platforms in home appliances, furniture, steel, plastic, hardware and construction materials, and machinery. The synergy works well, and most of the platforms in e-commerce are thriving.

Many companies from neighbouring Zhongshan, Nanhai and Nansha have moved their e-commerce operations to Shunde to take advantage of its holistic and evolving e-commerce environment. Some companies like Jinzheng even moved their manufacturing operations to Shunde as their online sales grew to a significant portion.

Biomedicine

Shunde's original biomedicine industry is relatively weak. Currently, only six pharmaceutical production companies are located there; two of them are domestic companies, and four are foreign companies. Leading companies like Guangdong Global Pharmaceutical and Guangdong Kangfulai Pharmaceutical mainly develop Chinese herbal medicine products.

There are 125 biotechnology companies, mostly domestic (107); leading companies like Foshan Shihezhong Biotechnology, Guangdong Houde Biotechnology mainly develop biological research reagents and clinical diagnostic products as well as monoclonal antibody drugs. Twenty-two companies focus on medical devices, and leading companies are Hisense Rongsheng (Guangdong) Freezer, Inteshकेng Medical Devices and Foshan Shunde Changxing Ultrasound Equipment. Twenty-two companies focus on health care products, and leading companies like Guangdong Yongzhengda Biotechnology, Foshan Shunde Heshengyuan Biotechnology and Huapeng Pharmaceutical Consulting focus on developing nutritional supplements and vitamins.

Shunde has two strategies to develop the biopharmaceuticals industry. The first involves the medical device industry and includes medical equipment, bio-pharmacy materials and diagnostics reagents. The second involves pharmacy production and consists of the production of drugs, antibiotics, vaccines, and so on. Since October 2015, 65 hectares of land in Lecong Town has been allocated to build Guangdong province's biopharmaceutical industrial park. The focus of the park is on attracting outstanding biomedical companies and institutions to settle there, introducing biomedicine talents, and creating a conducive environment to develop the industry.

During the first three quarters of 2018, five biomedical projects were brought into the area, and 25 projects were under negotiation. Projects range from medical devices, new drugs, biotechnology, big data projects, and so on. At the time of writing of this article, 35 biomedical projects have been set up, and total investment has exceeded 6.5 billion yuan. Some of these projects include a listing of a subsidiary company (Guangdong Anke Huanan Biotechnology), formation of two provincial innovation companies (Guangdong Bikang Biotechnology and Hanteng Biotechnology), and formation of three Foshan innovation companies (Foshan Hanteng Biotechnology, Shengmei Medical Technology (Guangdong), Guangdong Aishidai Biotechnology, and Guangdong Micro-decoding Biotechnology. Two companies are set up via a partnership with Germany (Foshan Hanteng Biotechnology and Foshan Pujin Biotechnology), and two with the United States (Foshan Baiao Express Medical Technology and Guangdong Shunde Xinnuo Wansi Biotechnology). There are also five Chinese academy projects.

Several biomedicine incubators have already been set up in Shunde. These include Jinan University Science and Technology Park (Shunde Park), Southern Medical University Science Park, International Innovation and Transformation Bio-industry Incubation Centre, and others. The current priority in the area is to attract talents and projects into the incubators.

Conclusion

Among Shunde's emerging industries, industrial design, tourism and modern exhibitions and e-commerce have made considerable progress.

Biopharmaceuticals, smart manufacturing and robotics remain in the nascent stage. However, Shunde will be working more closely with Shenzhen, a recognised leader in these areas, under the Greater Bay Area project. This collaboration will help in the development of these nascent high-tech industries. Bringing in KUKA as a strategic partner in robotics and smart manufacturing will also help.

In the past, Shunde successfully used its strong industrial manufacturing base to develop a foothold in the smart manufacturing and robotics industry. (For more details, see 'Shunde and the World Economy'.) Now, it is trying to repeat that success and continue building these strategic industries amid heightened competition and high barriers.

Chapter 11

Shunde's Industrial Parks and the Sino-German Industrial Services Zone

The manufacturing industry is the pillar of Shunde's economy, and it underpinned the spectacularly successful transformation of Shunde from an agricultural backwater to a bustling industrial city in the past 40 years. Industrial parks reflect a city's level of industrialisation; an old and dilapidated industrial park represents industrial backwardness, while a modern and well-run industrial park shows the dynamism of its industries.

Shunde is working to resolve the problems left behind by inefficient village-level industrial parks, while at the same time seeking upgrading and transformation through modern industrial parks. To address these issues, Shunde formulated a series of corresponding measures.

Consolidating and transforming village-level industrial parks

The earlier disorderly construction of village-level industrial parks was a consequence of Shunde's rapid development. In the 20th century, unplanned and poorly regulated factories proliferated in almost all villages at Shunde. These village-level industrial parks were dispersed around the whole district and occupied large tracts of land. They polluted heavily, and their output value was low; they occupied 70% of the designated industrial area, but their output was only 27% of the industrial sector. A host of other problems such as the illegal use of public land and overlapping property claims also made the parks hard to transform without government intervention.

While these poorly planned village-level industrial parks helped in the early industrialisation of Shunde when the place was short on funds, their continuing operation is now a drag on Shunde's development.

Based on the latest surveys, there are 382 village-level industrial parks in Shunde's 205 villages. Each village has an average of 1 to 2 village-level industrial parks occupying 9,000 hectares of land altogether. At the same time, many of these industrial parks had inadequate public infrastructure and did not have a master plan. Buildings were old and poorly built, safety hazards were aplenty, and it was often difficult to keep good social order in the zone. Many of them polluted the environment, negatively affecting the quality of life of residents and the city's landscape, and slowed down Shunde's urban development. Rejuvenation of the old village-level industrial parks and releasing of land for better use has been a challenge for Shunde.

In 2018, the Shunde government announced policy measures to transform these industrial parks under the 'Shunde Village-level Industrial Park Upgrading Proposal'. The proposal aims to consolidate the village-level industrial parks and turn them into modern industrial parks, and the projects are given top implementation priority.

Building three modern and innovative industrial parks

On the one hand, Shunde aims to promote its industrial development by transforming the village-level industrial parks and boosting their efficiency. On the other hand, it is also stepping up the building of new industrial parks to accelerate the attraction of emerging industries. Shunde is currently building three modern and innovative industrial parks: the Sino-German Industrial Services Zone, the Wisdom Valley of Southern China, and the New High-Tech Industrial Development Zone.

Sino-German Industrial Services Zone

The Sino-German Industrial Services Zone is an important international cooperation platform mandated by both the Chinese central government and the Guangdong provincial government. The Chinese and German prime ministers jointly agreed on its development in August 2012. It is a themed industrial park intended to serve as a collaboration platform.

The Sino-German Industrial Services Zone is also the first Sino-European urbanisation cooperation area. Urban upgrading is regarded as one of the critical complementary measures in the drive towards Guangdong's high-tech industrial transformation.

The Sino-German Industrial Services Zone holds significance at national, provincial and municipal levels. It spearheads Shunde's industrial upgrading and is the undisputed leader among the three new innovative industrial parks.

Wisdom Valley of Southern China

Wisdom Valley is located at the eastern edge of Shunde. It is designed to house company headquarters, high-end industry R&D centres as well as high-end service industries. Currently, Shunde New Energy Automobile Town, Lihe Shunde Science and Technology Park, Beijing University of Science and Technology Shunde Graduate School and other projects are in progress. Wisdom Valley will promote the development of urban-style industries and create a new science and technology cluster that integrates technological innovation, fintech and venture capital.

Shunde New High-Tech Industrial Development Zone

The new high-tech zone occupies a total area of 18.86 square kilometres and is at the western side of the district. It was identified as 'provincial-level high-tech development zone', 'provincial- and municipal-level base for the construction of a recycled economy', and the 'Guangdong intelligent manufacturing industry base'. By the end of 2017, the park has attracted 29 projects with a total investment worth 11.4 billion yuan.

The Sino-German Industrial Services Zone

The Sino-German Industrial Services Zone occupies a total area of 26 square kilometres. The plan is to build 666 hectares of smart manufacturing and high-tech industrial park which includes 200 hectares used for phase

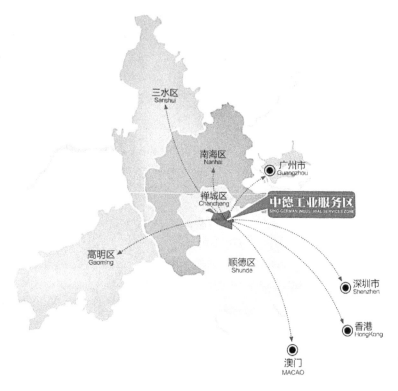

Figure 1. Location of the Sino-German Industrial Services Zone in Foshan

1 smart manufacturing cluster, 133 hectares each for future smart manufacturing cluster expansion as well as exhibition and convention space. The remaining 67 hectares are designated as a high-end residential town for professionals attracted to the Zone.

Three land transportation hubs and three waterway transportation hubs are being built in the Zone. Three subways lines (Foshan metro lines 3 and 6 and Guangfo Ring Line) and intercity transit lines such as Guangfo Jiangzhu intercity light rail will soon converge there.

Guangming and Foshan Yihuan expressways pass through the city, significantly reducing the distance between the Zone located in Foshan and Guangzhou. Only half an hour is needed to cover the 50 kilometres distance between the central and Guangzhou Baiyun International Airport while Foshan Airport is being used as a backup cargo and private airport. The Zone is accessible to any city in the Pearl River Delta within one hour by

Figure 2. Guangdong-Hong Kong-Macau Greater Bay Area

2030. Out of all of Shunde's industrial parks, the Zone's transportation linkage with the Greater Bay Area is most extensive and convenient.

The road network in Shunde takes a square-shaped framework, forming a 'seven horizontals and eight verticals' road structure. Connectivity within the district and with adjacent areas is excellent.

The Zone has three development goals: to promote cooperation between China and German high-tech companies, to facilitate an alliance between Chinese and German cities, and to demonstrate Sino-European urbanisation partnership.

Promoting cooperation between China and German high-tech companies

The high-tech industries focus on smart manufacturing, robotics, biomedical, as well as high-value producer services such as exhibitions and conventions. The Zone has consolidated resources in these priority areas and is in the process of optimising them to attract more investors. After development in recent years, the number of companies and projects that are currently in the Zone has exceeded 100.

The focus in smart manufacturing is on advanced industrial robots and automated production systems. The 80-hectare smart manufacturing industrial park jointly built by Midea and KUKA has commenced construction in the zone. Likewise, the largest civilian drone company in the world, DJI, has started a manufacturing operation. The Zone has also set up the Foshan Robotation Academy to train robotics professionals. The Foshan Robotation Academy is an authorised overseas partner institution of the Hannover Robotation Academy and is the first professional robotics training institute in China. The school has attracted 25 local and international institutions as partners; 14 are European, and 11 are Chinese. Hannover Robotation Academy will also carry out consulting work to assist companies in the adoption of robotics and automation technology.

The biomedical field focuses on the development of medical devices, precision medicine and medical diagnostic technology. The Zone has formed a partnership with the Chinese Academy of Sciences to build Guangdong Yuntian Bio-innovation Industry Centre; with Southern Medical University to develop a biopharmaceutical innovation base; and with Jinan University to build a biopharmaceutical industrial park.

The exhibition and convention industry is a high-end service industry. The Tanzhou International Convention & Exhibition Centre located inside the Zone focuses on professional exhibitions, R&D design, product validation and testing services, and vocational training. Leading global exhibition company Hannover Messe is a partner of the Tanzhou International Convention and Exhibition Centre. It has already held many large-scale exhibitions successfully. Among them, the China (Guandong) 'Internet +' Expo and Pearl River West Coast Advanced Equipment Manufacturing Investment Conference hold annual shows at the Tanzhou Exhibition Hall.

The Intelligent Science and Technology Park, Sino-European Centre, Tanzhou International Convention and Exhibition Centre and other industrial platforms are currently in operation, providing a stimulus to economic transformation in the region. The combination of the vast Chinese manufacturing base and German technology offers both quantitative and qualitative advantage to manufacturers in the Zone, allowing Foshan, Guangdong and even the whole country's manufacturing sector to grow.

Sino-German Industrial Service Alliance

The Sino-German Industrial Service Alliance was established in April 2017. It serves as an international cooperation platform jointly developed by important Chinese and German industrial cities. As of October 2018, the Alliance had 41 official members and observers. The number of Chinese official members, German official members, and Chinese observers are 21, 18, and two, respectively. China's Investment Promotion Agency of the Ministry of Commerce and Germany's Federal Foreign Trade and Investment Agency are the main sponsors of the Alliance. Other advisory organisations include the German North Rhine-Westphalia Investment Promotion Agency, the China Electronic Information Industry Development Research Institute, and the Guangdong Provincial Department of Commerce. The Alliance has now become an important networking platform for China and Germany.

The Secretariat and German Liaison Office are responsible for the Alliance's operations. The Secretariat is located at the Sino-German Industrial Services Zone and the German Liaison Office in Berlin and Dusseldorf. Working committees under the secretariat are also set up to facilitate the exchange of technical information.

The Alliance actively facilitates economic and trade exchanges, corporate mergers and acquisitions, and technical cooperation between Chinese and German member cities. It has successfully promoted about 50 cases, including the partnership between Midea and KUKA, and settling the Aachen Industry 4.0 Technology Application Research Centre in Shunde.

The Alliance focuses on five working areas that relate to economic and trade development, industrial cooperation, personnel training, mutual financial assistance, and cultural exchange.

It has already attracted Hannover Messe, the Hannover Robotation Academy, the Fraunhofer Association, Aachen University of Technology, and other institutions to invest and operate in Shunde. These institutions possess world-class experts in their fields, and they have brought advanced technology and management to China. The Hannover Exhibition, Guangdong International 'Internet +' Expo and other events are held every year. These activities provide a regular cooperation platform for its member cities.

The Alliance regularly arranges for Chinese business, economic and trade missions to visit Germany. For small- and medium-sized companies, it also organises study tours to Germany for the entrepreneurs and their second-generation successors.

In the first half of 2018, the Alliance conducted more than 60 trips to Germany for nearly 50 corporations. It promoted cooperation between Germany's Asklepios Group (the country's largest medical group) and Shunde's Guangyi Medical Technology Co., as well as between Germany's Augsburg Football Club and Shunde's Football Association. The German Machinery Industry Future Alliance (ZAM) also set up an office at Foshan, the mother city of Shunde.

The Alliance has helped Chinese companies such as Yizumi, Hongshi Laser and Liansu Group to set up subsidiaries in Germany, find German partners, carry out joint R&D, and invest in M&A. These activities are in addition to the regular consulting services it provides to local businesses that are keen to learn about Germany.

The Sino-German Industrial Service Alliance plays an essential role in the bilateral exchange between China and Germany.

Sino-European urbanisation partnership

The Sino-German Industrial Services Zone is one of the first development areas used to demonstrate urbanisation cooperation between China and Europe. Germany is known for its planning and construction standards, and many German cities have earned the nickname '100-year-city' because of its sturdy construction and timeless design that can last 100 years while not being outdated. By integrating the design spirit with urban development needs, an urbanisation development approach that is intelligent, green, low-carbon and ecological sound can be developed and adopted for Chinese need.

The Sino-German Industrial Services Zone promotes green buildings. At present, all new buildings in its core area are considered green, and buildings along the periphery that are ranked two stars and above have reached more than 30%. Regarding sponge city construction (a concept of full water-recycling capability), 80% of the rainwater in the core area is recycled and used. In the green municipal district, a 12-kilometre integrated water piping system has been built, and tap water in the core area has reached the European drinking water standard. The Sino-European urbanisation partnership has earned a favourable image for the Sino-German Industrial Services Zone, and the Zone won the 'CEIBS Green and Smart City

Excellence Award' and 'CEIBS Green and Smart City Technology Innovation Award' in 2015 and 2016 respectively.

In terms of the green environment, the riverside environmental project has an 8-kilometre long riverside corridor consisting of walking galleries along the bank, open-air swimming pools, water parks, dragon boat plazas and leisure sports facilities.

The Sino-German urbanisation partnership has become a model for urban ecological design in the Pearl River Delta. The design significantly contributed to Foshan being awarded the title 'National Forest City'.

The area possesses first-class public facilities like cultural centres, a sports centre, a performing arts centre, a hospital, a book city and a cinema. Together with a comprehensive transportation network of subway, light rail and buses, a high quality and full coverage public service system is made available. Currently, the science museum, youth centre, library, archives centre, grand theatre and urban planning exhibition hall have been opened to the public.

The intelligent robotic machinery manufacturing arm

Robots and smart manufacturing are closely related, and they share a lot of standard technologies. Most of the players in these two industries are different divisions of the same companies.

China has been the world's largest and fastest-growing market for robots since 2013. It accounts for 1/3 of the global robotics market in recent years. Domestically, the robotic industry is also one of the country's fastest-growing sector; in 2017, it was worth 120 billion yuan, a year-on-year increase of 25.4%.

In 2017, the ratio between robots and workers was 88:10,000, surpassing the 80:10,000 average of the world's industrial countries for the first time. However, compared to the 150:10,000 ratio in most industrialised countries, China is still in the catch-up phase.

As China's industrial robotics industry is a latecomer and just took off in the last ten years, the market is currently dominated by multinational robotics companies. In the '2018 China Robot Industry Analysis Report', the Harbin Institute of Technology Robotics Group and China Science and Technology Evaluation and Research Centre pointed out problems relating to three robotics fields.

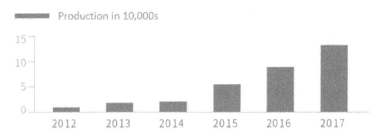

Figure 3. Chinese robot production from 2012 to 2017 (in 10,000s)

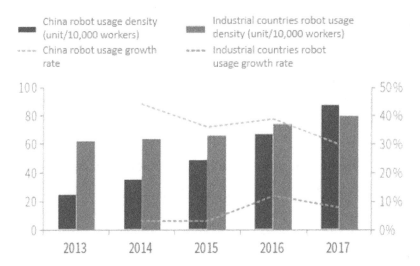

Figure 4. Robot application density for China and industrial countries from 2013 to 2017

Firstly, the core components of industrial robots rely on imports, and it is difficult to reduce production cost. The country is weak in translating university or research institute work to commercially viable products. The industry standards on robotics are not comprehensive, and quality of products vary. Most companies rely on government policy to stay viable. Secondly, service robots face problems in key technology breakthroughs, high prices, and poor records on functionality and safety. These problems slowed down the adoption of service robots in service businesses. Thirdly, companies that manufacture specialised robots face high technology barriers and have difficulty staying viable.

The report also highlights that the current Chinese robotics industry has several tailwinds favourable to its development. First are the favourable government policies that support their growth, economic environment (robots replacing humans), social environment (corporate awareness and social acceptance) and technical environment. The domestic supply chain of the industrial robot industry has improved in the last few years, and localisation of core components is gaining momentum. The service robot market has taken off, and some leading manufacturers are becoming profitable. Specialised robots are in the nascent stage, and bionic technology has become the focus of its R&D.

The structure of China's robot industry is different from other countries. Based on 2017's industrial output value for the 435 companies engaged in the robot assembly operation, industrial robots, service robots and specialised robots accounted for 26.6 billion (61%), 12.2 billion (28%) and 4.7 billion (11%) respectively. In other countries, industrial robots take up almost the entire market. Suzhou Ecovacs, China's leading and one of the world's largest robot cleaner manufacturing company, recorded 4.551 billion yuan in revenue and 376 million yuan in net profit in 2017.

Midea and KUKA's joint Smart Manufacturing Industrial Park is designed to bring together robotics and smart manufacturing companies, as well as their related upstream and downstream supply chain companies, to build a viable ecosystem for these two industries. The park plans to invest 10 billion yuan in the Sino-German Industrial Services Zone. It is the Zone's

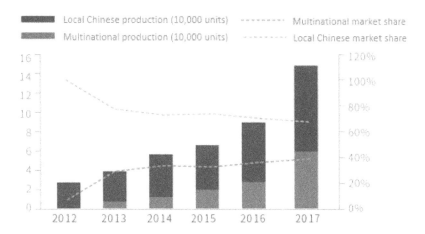

Figure 5. Sales of Chinese industrial robots from 2012 to 2017

core project and involves the construction of smart manufacturing factories, office and R&D areas, exhibition centres, and accommodation for talents. The park will house four major business segments: smart manufacturing, smart logistics, smart healthcare, and smart homes. Midea is an early adopter of smart manufacturing in China and has accumulated many years of experience to deal with the complexity of technology integration in the production line, while KUKA is a global leader in the field of robotics and automation. Their resources are complementary and synergistic, and the Midea-KUKA joint venture will serve as the anchor of Shunde's drive in smart manufacturing and robotics.

Currently, the number of industrial robot companies in Foshan is around 100. Between January and June 2018, Foshan companies bought 1,626 new industrial robots. Among Shunde's manufacturers, more than 180 companies use industrial robots now. The end-user market of robots and smart manufacturing at Shunde is vibrant and growing.

Conclusion

Robotics and smart manufacturing system industries have a high technological threshold, and they call for systems integration of various disciplines. Successful development must be based on a solid technical foundation and cooperation with advanced enterprises.

With support from the Greater Bay Area project, the presence of the Sino-German Industrial Services Zone will help Shunde become an important robot production base in China, next to Shanghai. Shenzhen is a major robotics development town in Southern China and is the home base for reputable robotics companies like Huichuan Technology. The integration of the Greater Bay Area facilitates the cooperation of industries between Shunde and Shenzhen.

Shunde encourages its traditional manufacturers to upgrade and transform their operations by promoting the use of smart manufacturing technologies and equipment like robots. The 'Internet + Intelligent Manufacturing' upgrading project at 100 companies, 'smart factories' project are also currently underway to promote the two cornerstone industrial clusters — home appliances and machinery.

Chapter 12

Shunde's Business Environment

Since the reform and opening up, Shunde has continuously built an excellent business environment. In the late 1970s, Shunde pioneered township enterprises and the 'three-plus-one' cooperative trade enterprises. In 1987, Shunde took the lead in delegating four management rights, namely personnel management, institutional setup, internal distribution and product Pricing, to the company. From 1992 to 2018, Shunde was selected four times as a reform pilot county by the central government and Guangdong province. In 1992, a series of comprehensive reforms focusing on property rights was introduced. In 1999, Shunde was the first pilot city in China to experiment on means to become a modern city and to build a service-oriented government suitable for the market economy. In 2009, Shunde implemented a large-scale administrative reform to streamline government operations further. In 2018, Shunde was chosen as a 'high-quality administrative development and innovative reform experimental zone'. The main content of each reform included improving the business environment in Shunde.

The excellent business environment has cultivated a large number of outstanding local enterprises and has also attracted business from all localities to invest in Shunde. The number of enterprises in Shunde increased from about 2,000 state-owned or collectively owned enterprises in 1978 to 218,132 at the end of October 2018, among which 103,083 were domestic-funded enterprises (97% or more are private enterprises), 2,520 were foreign-funded enterprises (of which nearly 50 were established by 28 Fortune 500 companies), 112,456 were sole proprietorships and 73 are farmers' cooperatives. In April 2018, Shunde had an average of 1,350 new domestic-funded enterprises per month, ranking high in the country in terms of the regional population.

There are more than 12,000 manufacturing factories in the region, with large, medium and small enterprises coexisting with one another. They include Midea — a world's top 500 company with annual sales of more than 200 billion yuan, 73 benchmark private enterprises with annual sales exceeding 1 billion yuan, as well as numerous family-owned spare parts manufacturers. Private enterprises accounted for nearly 80% of the industrial output value of large-scale enterprises.

The flourishing development of private enterprises and the coexistence and co-prosperity of large, medium and small enterprises in Shunde illustrate the success of Shunde's excellent business environment.

To examine the business environment of a region, the following factors are considered: government economic policies and corporate support policies; supply and costs of production factor, industrial clusters, and market conditions.

Government economic policy

In the past, the Shunde people implemented the integrated mulberry tree and fish pond agronomy model. From there, they accumulated knowledge of the cash commodity economy, and understood the importance of the business environment in the market economy. This economic and cultural gene flourished after the reform and opening up. (See 'Shunde's Innovations' for details).

In the early days of the reform, Shunde took the lead in promoting the 'three-plus-one' cooperative trade enterprises and township enterprises. Shunde, an agricultural county with no money, no technology and no talent at that time, took the first step in exploring the business environment. The people of Shunde have a consensus — economic development must be carried out by the whole district, and it has never changed in the past 40 years. The strategy of industrial-led development and focusing on key enterprises established in the early days of Shunde's reform has not changed.

In recent years, Shunde is adapting to the new economic environment and promulgating economic policies to support emerging industries. Through the creation of innovative systems, increased investment in scientific research, the establishment of industry-university-research platforms, public platforms, Technology Shunde, and tax incentives, Shunde wants to encourage and foster corporate innovation capabilities and enterprise growth. (See 'Shunde's Emerging Industries' and 'Shunde's Industrial Parks' for more details.)

Shunde's government and its services have been praised by entrepreneurs for years. The reform of the administrative approval system in Shunde started from the 1992 reform of the administrative system. In 2011, the Shunde government again took the lead in launching a new round of administrative approval system reform among the county towns. Both series of reform were at the forefront of the country. In 2015, Shunde followed Foshan to develop a one-stop service for enterprise registration, business license and investment construction. This service is in operation now and dramatically reduces the approval time for enterprise registration and investment construction. At present, Shunde is stepping up the reform of the one-stop service and creating a digital-enabled government.

Foshan city takes the lead in implementing a 365-day 24-hour business registration service. Through the self-service terminal, a new company can be registered via paperless submission, one-time review and on-site instant registration. A business license can be obtained in 5 minutes.

In 2018, Shunde district implemented an approval service that does not require face-to-face meetings and a government service model that promised dealings are approved in one go. The focus is on advancing service-oriented government functions and improving the business environment.

Shunde's excellent business environment has attracted entrepreneurs. In 2017, Shunde attained 121 projects with each investment exceeding 100 million yuan (with more than 10 million US dollars in foreign capital), with a total investment of 131.367 billion yuan; 28 projects with each investment exceeding 1 billion yuan, with a total investment of 94.967 billion yuan. The number of investments of over 100 million yuan and over 1 billion yuan is the highest among the five districts of Foshan.

In the 2018 China Credit Health Index, the China Business Environment Satisfaction Survey introduced the newly-launched China Top 100 Business Districts and Counties, in which Shunde was ranked seventh in the country, only lagging behind Nanshan district in Shenzhen in the whole of Guangdong province.

Table 1. Services provided by Shunde government

Departments	No. of services that do not require face-to-face meetings	No. of services in which dealings are approved in one go
District Administration and Planning Bureau (Development Reform Statistics)	4	4
District Environmental Management Bureau (Environmental Protection)	8	10
District and Municipal Supervision (Industrial and Commercial Quality Supervision)	7	4
District and Municipal Supervision (Food and Drug Administration)	2	6
District Health and Welfare Bureau	2	42
District Public Security Bureau	4	—
District Justice Bureau	—	21
District Tax Department	82	—
District Civil Affairs and Human Resources Social Security Administration	—	81
District Meteorological Bureau	—	4

In September 2018, Shunde was chosen as a 'high-quality administrative development and innovative reform experimental zone', creating a first-class business environment was one of the important contents. Today, Shunde is preparing to launch a new round of administrative approval system reform.

Supply and costs of production factors

The supply and costs of production factors are the most important factors determining the success or failure of enterprises. Shunde district has been continuously improving the supply conditions and controlling the costs of production factors. At present, Shunde's production factor prices are at a medium level in the whole of the Guangdong-Hong Kong-Macau Greater Bay Area.

In terms of human resources, Shunde has established a multi-level talent supply system to provide a good human resources environment. Shunde is utilising migrant workers to solve the problem of insufficient local labour, and is also controlling labour costs and continuously improving the cultural quality of the workforce.

In the multi-level talent supply system, the middle, tertiary and post-graduate education institutions of Shunde can provide more than 13,500 higher- and middle-educated vocational technicians every year. At the same time, Shunde's vocational education is tightly integrated with the strong manufacturing industry. Professional courses can be adapted based on the needs of enterprises.

Shunde is close to Guangzhou, and talent resources from the surrounding areas can be accessed to supplement the gap in local high-end talents. Foshan has seven normal colleges, six adult colleges, three higher vocational and technical colleges, 40 middle vocational and technical colleges, with a total of 150,000 students. At the same time, due to its location advantage, Shunde can also share the talent resources of nearly 20,000 graduate students and 250,000 college students in 37 colleges and universities in Guangzhou.

At the same time, the 'Satellite City' of Guangzhou University is being built in the northern part of Shunde. It aims to establish a talent cooperation mechanism with ten well-known higher learning institutions at home and abroad, establish 100 innovative platforms to integrate the financial and technological industries, attract more than 1,000 talents with leadership potential and attract more than 10,000 high-end talents (master's graduates or senior executives).

The Foshan Robotation Academy, which is newly established in the Sino-German Industrial Services Zone, and the Guangdong Aachen Industry 4.0 Technology Application Research Centre, are nurturing talents for Shunde to promote emerging industries such as smart manufacturing, industrial robots and future equipment manufacturing.

To provide a excellent human resources environment, Shunde Talent Development Service Centre actively builds a variety of labour employment platforms and regularly organises on-site job fairs in the region to provide recruitment platforms for enterprises and reduce recruitment costs. In 2016, the Talent Development Service Centre held 70 job fairs, and about

2,980 companies participated in the recruitment, with an attendance of about 110,000 people.

The Shunde Talent Development Service Centre also sends a Shunde delegation to universities outside the district to encourage fresh graduates to visit Shunde to explore the employment opportunities.

Shunde has 19 re-employment training institutions to carry out skills training for more than 50 types of work. In 2016, more than 60,000 people participated in vocational skills training.

In recent years, Shunde has successively launched high-level industries, medical and health systems, and the identification and importing of educational talents to provide convenience for enterprises to employ high-level talents. By the end of 2017, Shunde has attracted 6,956 high-level industrial talents, including 151 first-, second-, and third-class talents; 3,361 high-level education talents, including 56 first-, second-, and third-class talents; and 1,953 high-level health personnel, including seven first-, second-, and third-class talents.

Faced with the shortage of local labour force, Shunde began to introduce migrant workers in the 1990s to control the rising labour costs. At present, indigenous residents and 'new Shunde people' (migrant workers) each account for half of the labour force. By the end of 2017, the number of highly-skilled migrant talents in Shunde reached 64,000. The talent structure is continuously optimised, and the types of work have gradually changed to electricians, mould workers, CNC lathe workers, CNC milling machine workers and others.

Shunde's per capita GDP is at the upper-middle level of the Pearl River Delta. However, Shunde effectively controls labour costs through the

Table 2. Comparison of wages and per capita GDP in major regions of the Pearl River Delta

	Average annual salary of employees in 2015 (yuan)	2016 per capita GDP (yuan)
Guangzhou	81168	45254.30
Shenzhen	81034	171304.70
Foshan	61810	116141.30
Shunde	63239	118597.00
Dongguan	53220	82718.53

Table 3. Payments to various social security items in 2018

Insurance type	Wage (yuan/month)	Company payment ratio	Individual payment ratio
Endowment insurance	3100–20004	13%	8%
Unemployment Insurance	1720–18177	0.5%	0.2%
Work injury insurance	3635–18177	0.2-1.3%	—
Medical insurance	5599	4%	0.5-1.5%
Maternity insurance	4544–18177	0.5%	—
Total		18.2–19.3%	8.7%-9.7%
Minimum wage standard (2018)		1720	

Table 4. Education level of workers in Foshan City

Education level	Every 100,000 labour force in 2000	Every 100,000 labour force in 2010	Growth rate
High school (including vocational high school, technical school and vocational middle school) and above	19378	20065	3.54%
College and above	9469	14142	49.35%

introduction of migrant technicians and implementation of social security payment ratios. Compared to other cities in the Pearl River Delta, Shunde's salary is at a medium level.

Shunde continuously improves the cultural quality of the labour force. According to the government of Foshan city, the average education period of the working-age population is 12 years, the proportion of workers with higher education is over 20%, and the average education period of new labour is 14 years.

As for other production factors such as industrial land use fees, industrial electricity charges, water fees, and so on, Shunde's costs are similar to the industrial cities around the Pearl River Delta. However, Shunde's policies have flexibility, especially for land use fees.

When confirming a land bid, the Shunde government generally formulates the final land price based on the industrial direction of the investment project, environmental impact, energy consumption indicators, investment plans, economic benefits, investor credibility in conjunction with land transfer criteria. For high-quality projects with large industrial driving effects and obvious economic and social benefits, Shunde will formulate land prices according to the specific conditions of the project.

Industrial cluster situation

The modern industry emphasises the division of labour, and the degree of interdependence between upstream and downstream enterprises is increasing. An excellent industrial cluster can effectively improve economies of scale, reduce costs, promote the speed of technological innovation, offset rising R&D costs and reduce increased R&D pressure brought about by technological advancements. Shunde's eight pillar industries (household appliances, machinery and equipment, information and communications technology, fine chemicals, furniture manufacturing, packaging and printing, bio-pharmaceuticals and textiles and garments) are famous for their great industrial clusters, while the six pillar industries (except bio-pharmaceuticals and textiles and garments) are closely interdependent and interlocked. Emerging industries that Shunde wants to support and encourage, such as smart manufacturing, robotics and e-commerce trade, are related to the current pillar industries. (For details, see the article 'The Shunde Economic Phenomenon'.) These favourable conditions are an important attraction for investors.

Market situation

The transportation network in and outside of Shunde is quite developed. It is thus very convenient for the transportation of goods out of the district, regardless of sea, land or air (for details, please refer to the article 'Shunde: A General Introduction). Shunde led the country into international trade through the 'three-plus-one' cooperative trade enterprises in the 1980s. Hence, the business community in Shunde is in a comparatively advantageous position in China, as they are armed with knowledge of integrating into the international market, promoting international business cooperation, and protecting intellectual property rights. At the same time, Shunde's home appliances and furniture industries, which were developed in the 1990s, also occupy leading positions in the market. The Shunde government and entrepreneurs have understood and mastered the domestic and foreign markets, and have created an excellent business environment for Shunde.

High standards to improve the business environment

Shunde is once again acting as a leader in improving the business environment. Shunde has benchmarked itself with World Bank standards and is striving towards the goal of having a first-class business environment. It is aiming to be the best and the most advanced in both domestic and international markets, further delineate the boundaries of market and government, create a fair and efficient government, and build an open, active and orderly market environment. It is also aiming to attract high-quality industries, enterprises and talents to Shunde by developing an international, legalised and convenient business environment.

The '1121' programme launched in 2018 took the first big step in the whole of China towards a streamlined and lean government. Under the '1121' programme, Shunde is working on creating a business environment with the least approvals, the shortest process time and the best service. The programme wants to set up a trust approval model of 'clear policy, corporate credibility and effective supervision'. Specifically, general industrial projects approval would only need 11 working days, including registration of project to the acquisition of construction permits (excluding public announcement, project reviews, hearings and other special procedures), to complete; housing construction projects approval would only take up to 21 working days to complete.

Shunde proposes to strengthen the rule of law in the business environment by building a nation-leading intellectual property protection system. Works to be done include setting up intellectual property circuit courts and procuratorates, enhancing IP custody and risk warning, improving government management and services with big data, and building a coordinated management and service mechanism across systems, departments and services in the government.

Conclusion

Shunde is working towards improving its business environment by analysing the actual situation, borrowing from past experience, and benchmarking itself with the country's and the world's leading standards. Shunde will continuously optimise its business environment and provide a good foundation for future economic development. Currently, Shunde's emerging industries are facing the shortage of a large number of high-level talents. Through the implementation of the Guangdong-Hong Kong-Macau Greater Bay Area, there will be in-flow of high-level talents, thereby helping to improve Shunde's business environment.

Chapter 13

Prominent Companies from Shunde

Shunde is primarily an industrial city, and its industrial production accounts for more than 55% of the local GDP. Household appliances production accounts for 15% of the country's total. It is prominent in the country in terms of the strength of its home appliances and furniture clusters, and the number of national famous brands. Private enterprises account for 80% of Shunde's industrial production and are among the highest in the country's important industrial cities. Since the advent of China's reform and opening up, until Shunde's establishment as a production bastion, there have been many famous private enterprises founded by legendary entrepreneurs. Many of these founders started out as peasant entrepreneurs in township enterprises before China's opening up. They have built national and even global enterprises with their hard work and perseverance.

Midea Group and He Xiangjian

Midea Group is the benchmark for Shunde's manufacturing and home appliances industries. On the Fortune 500 Global List 2018, Midea ranks at number 323 with 2017 sales of 240 billion yuan and group net profit of 17.3 billion yuan. At present, the company has 12 strategic business units, 150,000 employees at home and abroad, nearly 200 subsidiaries, more than 60 overseas branches, and 20 research institutes around the world. In 2007, the group set up its first overseas production base in Vietnam. Currently, there are six foreign production bases in Vietnam, India, Egypt, Belarus, Brazil and Argentina. Also, there are 12 domestic production bases distributed nationwide. Midea's overseas sales account for 45% of its total sales. Midea Group is the leader in the internationalisation of Shunde's enterprises. Its foreign investment amount exceeds 5 billion US dollars, accounting for the vast majority of the 6.285 billion US dollars overseas investment amount approved by Shunde district.

In 1968, He Xiangjian led 23 people to raise 5,000 yuan to set up the 'Beijie Office Plastic Production Group' in Beijiao, Shunde and produced plastic bottle caps in the form of a village-run enterprise. In 1980, it began to produce electric fans and entered the home appliances industry. In 1981, it officially registered the 'Midea' trademark. In 1985, it began to manufacture air-conditioning products. In 1992, Midea became the first township enterprise to be approved by the China Securities Regulatory Commission to be listed on the Shenzhen Stock Exchange under the name 'Guangdong Midea'. After public listing, the company's primary business income grew rapidly from 487 million yuan in 1992 to 2.5 billion yuan in 1996, entering the ranks of China's largest home appliances manufacturers. In 2000, the company's sales amounted to 10 billion yuan; in 2010, it further broke through 100 billion yuan and realised the miracle of ten times sales growth in ten years. In 2012, He Xiangjian, the chairman of the company, resigned and was replaced by professional manager Fang Hongbo. In 2013, the group was reorganised, and its listing status was transferred from Guangdong Midea to its parent company, Midea Group. Midea Group is considered by the securities market to be a company with modern corporate management capabilities, and nearly 20% of its shares are held by international institutional investors.

Table 1. Major indicators of Midea Group, 2017

	Sales (100 million yuan)	Percentage
Sales	2407	100
Manufacturing	2211	91.9
Air conditioning equipment	954	39.6
Consumer electronics	987	41.0
Robotics and automation equipment	270	11.2
Domestic sales amount	1368	56.8
Overseas sales amount	1040	43.2

Table 2. Midea's product market share

Leading product	Market position
Air conditioner	Domestic second
Washing machine	Domestic second
Refrigerator	Domestic third
Rice cooker	Domestic first, world first
Induction cooker	Domestic first, world first
Electric pressure cooker	Domestic first, world first
Electric kettle	Domestic first, world first
Microwave oven	Domestic second, world third
Water heater	Domestic third
Hood	Domestic third

In terms of brand awareness, Midea ranked number 26 in the BrandZ^{TM} Top 100 Most Valuable Chinese Brands in 2018, and it has been the highest-ranking home appliances brand in China for three consecutive years. The company is one of the top 10 companies and also one of the top 10 public companies in China Central Television's National Brands Plan in 2018.

Many of Midea's products have a leading position in both domestic and foreign markets, as seen in Table 2.

Midea Group played an important role in the industrial transformation and upgrading of Shunde district. The company invested 8.5 billion yuan in research in 2017. The company has 500 doctoral researchers in Shunde, accounting for about 1/3 of the 1600 doctorates in Shunde district. Midea's research spending is 3.5% of sales, which is significantly higher than the average of 2.4% among peers in the industry in Shunde.

In 2016, the company acquired German-based KUKA — one of the world's top four robotics companies. It has also established joint laboratories with domestic and foreign scientific research institutions, such as the Chinese Academy of Sciences, Tsinghua University, MIT, UC Berkeley, Stanford University and Purdue University to build a global innovation ecosystem.

According to International Clarivate Analytics' *The State of Innovation 2017*, Midea is a leader in invention patents in the home appliances industry. In 2017, Midea applied for 16,934 patents in China, including 7,714 invention patents. By the end of 2017, Midea had applied for more than 70,000 patents. It currently has 35,000 patents.

Table 3. Number of patents of the world's top ten home appliances manufacturers, 2016

Company	Country	No of patents
Midea	China	5040
Gree	China	2567
Haier	China	1732
Mitsubishi Electric	Japan	944
LG	South Korea	866
Panasonic	Japan	806
BSH Hausgeraete	Germany	760
Joyoung	China	631
Samsung	South Korea	444
Hisense	China	429

Table 4. Midea's offline and online home appliances market share and ranking

Product	Offline market share	Ranking	Online market share	Ranking
Air conditioner	24.6%	2	24%	2
Washing machine	24.6%	2	29%	1
Refrigerator	10.7%	3	15%	2
Rice cooker	44.8%	1	33%	1
Pressure cooker	47.7%	1	—	—
Induction cooker	52.5%	1	42%	1
Electric kettle	—	—	25%	1
Electric fan and electric stove	45.0%	1	21%	1
Clothing steam engine	—	—	30%	1
Microwave oven	45.3%	2	—	—
Electric oven	—	—	21%	1
Water filter	23.1%	2	12%	3
Water heater	19.6%	3	34%	1
Gas water heater	11.4%	3	21%	1
Hob	7.0%	4	—	—
Range hood	8.5%	4	17%	1
Air to water heat pump	—	—	38%	1
Drinking fountain	—	—	30%	1

Midea is one of the earliest home appliances companies in China to enter the e-commerce market. In 2017, the domestic online sales amount of Midea was about 40 billion yuan, accounting for 30% of sales. It is the brand with the highest market share in the online home appliances sector.

Besides its automobile and electronics industries, China's home appliances industry is another industry that uses robots extensively. It is also the first Chinese industry to try to enter the realm of automated unmanned factories. Midea's investment in this area is particularly significant. In recent years, through cooperation with the Japanese robot manufacturer Yaskawa and the successful acquisition of KUKA, Midea has already begun to show some results. Its subsidiary Annto's automatic guided vehicle (AGV) is a leader in the automated logistics industry. Midea started the construction of the Midea-KUKA Intelligent Manufacturing Base in 2018 and this base is expected to form an industrial cluster worth 100 billion yuan for the region.

The success of Midea Group in the home appliances industry has made the company a model for the home appliances industry in Shunde. The company's overseas expansion model has also been emulated by other companies in Shunde. Midea Group's 'Smart Home + Smart Manufacturing' development strategy has been adopted by Shunde district as a blueprint for the development of the home appliances industry. Midea has become an important corporate member of the Shunde district government's economic development strategy known as 'Technology Shunde'.

He Xiangjian, born in 1942, is the most famous farmer entrepreneur from Shunde. With his hard work and perseverance, wisdom of making good use of talents (see the article 'Shunde and the World Economy' for details) and philosophy of 'change is the only constant', He Xiangjian vigorously promoted the reform of the internal shareholding system of the company, thereby enabling Midea to become the first listed company that was reorganised from a township enterprise. He also actively implemented the segregation of shareholders, the board of directors and management team, and created a precedent for the reform of private enterprise equity, equity incentives, professional managers and modern enterprise. He also established a charitable fund by investing more than 10 billion yuan and used the fund to carry out philanthropic causes such as poverty alleviation, disaster relief, pension, education, etc. For this, He Xiangjian won the title of 'National Model Worker,' among others.

On November 26, 2018, the central government celebrated the 40th anniversary of China's reform and opening up. In the list of 100 outstanding contributors to the reform and opening up, there are 9 people from Guangdong, including two from Foshan city. He Xiangjian, a forerunner in restructuring and listing TVEs on the stock exchange, is awarded a Reform Pioneer medal.

Country Garden and Yang Guoqiang

Country Garden is another 200-billion-yuan enterprise from Shunde. On the Fortune 500 Global List 2018, Country Garden ranks at number 353 with 2017 sales of 227 billion yuan and net profit of 26.1 billion yuan. In 2017, the company sold 60 million square metres of completed real estate (both wholly-owned and joint ventures), with a total sales of 550.8 billion. It is one of the largest real estate developers in China and the world.

Country Garden and Midea are both located in Beijiao, Shunde, and they are the only two 200-billion-yuan enterprises in Shunde. The GDP of Beijiao began to surpass Shunde's traditionally most affluent locale, Ronggui, in 2013, and these two companies contributed a lot to this achievement.

The company has completed 1,500 real estate projects worldwide, and its property companies manage more than 3 million homes. At the end of 2017, the company has 1,468 projects in progress, covering 30 provinces, 220 cities and 768 towns and districts in China.

Country Garden's tagline is 'Give you a five-star home'. The company emphasises that its properties, environment, facilities, property management, and corporate culture all attain industry-leading five-star standards. Country Garden is famous in the real estate industry for its large-scale new district development and high concentration of internal resources. It provides a one-stop service ranging from property landscaping, interior design, after-sales property management and building materials.

Country Garden is listed on the main board of the Hong Kong Stock Exchange since 2007. In recent years, the company has entered the field of industrial villages development and has carried out the development of new energy vehicle towns and robot development zones in Shunde. The company hires highly educated, postdoctoral staff to enter these new fields. Currently, it employs nearly 600 such talents, ranking first among Shunde enterprises.

Country Garden's founder Yang Guoqiang, is another well-known peasant entrepreneur from Shunde. He is from a poor family, and it is said that he only wore his first pair of shoes when he was 17 years old. Yang Guoqiang started as a construction contractor. In one of his construction projects, he took over from a developer who had a bad project. He provided the land for free to a prestigious middle school and brought the project back to life. He is a pioneer in large-scale real estate development using a school-home combination: Yang Guoqiang's professionalism and passion for his work are well-known in the industry.

Yang Guoqiang attaches great importance to education and has established many free charity schools such as Guohua Memorial Middle School and Guangdong Country Garden Vocational College. In October 2018, Yang Guoqiang donated 2.2 billion yuan to Tsinghua University, the most significant single contribution since the establishment of the university.

Galanz and Liang Qingde

Founded in 1978, Galanz was formerly a township factory specialising in down products. In 40 years, the small township factory started by seven people has developed into a multinational white goods group with nearly 50,000 employees. In 2017, its sales of 21 billion yuan ranked it 269th in the top 500 Chinese private enterprises. Galanz was selected as one of the top 100 Chinese brands in 2017 and ranked 46th.

Galanz is the leader in the production of microwave ovens and electric ovens. Galanz's microwave oven ranks first in China and third in the world; it ranks second in China and second in the world in the electric oven market. In the China Brand Power Index ranking, Galanz maintained its number one position in the microwave oven industry from 2011 to 2017 and was awarded the 'Golden Brand' award. Its customer satisfaction and customer referral indexes maintained their leading positions as well.

Galanz's steady development and growth in the past 40 years is a testament to the success of China's reform and opening up. In its first ten years, Galanz started from scratch to create a textile industry worth over 100 million yuan. In the second ten years, Galanz moved from the textile industry to the microwave oven industry, becoming one of the first township enterprises in China to successfully transform into a modern enterprise, and it also became the world leader in the microwave oven market. In the third ten years, Galanz began to build a multinational white goods group with microwave ovens, air conditioners, refrigerators, washing machines and household appliances as its core. In the fourth decade, Galanz invested more than 3 billion yuan in upgrading to smart production and promoted the automation of the entire industrial chain. In particular, Galanz imported from Europe an automatic production line for dishwashers with an annual production capacity of 1 million units; invested nearly 100 million yuan to launch a world-class drum and box production line; launched the world's first automatic assembly line for microwave ovens; and launched the world's first automatic electric steam furnace production line.

Galanz possesses a full range of technology to produce white goods. It has independent research and development and professional manufacturing capabilities to produce household appliances such as microwave ovens, electric ovens, electric steamers, refrigerators, air conditioners, washing machines and dishwashers, and components and parts such as control tubes, compressors, transformers and computer boards. Galanz is the leader in the industry in terms of automation and R&D.

Galanz is another exemplar of the internationalisation of Shunde's enterprises. Since the 1990s, the company has been active in attending exhibitions around the world and has established a wide range of strategic partnerships with global retailers. It has adopted a very pragmatic brand development model — the '5+1' model. The '5' refers to cooperative brands, joint venture brands, rental brands, and cooperation with top international brands from standard OEM to ODM. The '1' refers to its self-owned brand. Galanz has established subsidiaries, R&D centres and business branches in the United States, Germany, the United Kingdom, Japan, Chile, Spain, Russia, India, Vietnam, Australia, the United Arab Emirates and other countries and regions. It has also set up localised marketing teams to increase the global brand of Galanz. As of 2017, Galanz has applied for 2,498 domestic and international patents and has registered independent trademarks in 138 countries and regions around the world.

Liang Qingde is the founder of Galanz. Born in 1937, he is also a famous farmer entrepreneur. He started three businesses. In 1978, he founded the Shunde Guizhou Down Factory; in 1988, he founded the Guizhou Animal Products Enterprise (Group) Company; in June 1992, he founded Guangdong Galanz Enterprise (Group) Co., Ltd. His entrepreneurial story has become the stuff of legend. In the early days of Galanz, he seized the opportunity to move into the microwave oven industry in 1992 with the '5+1' model. In 13 years, he set up 19 production lines around the world and established cooperation with 250 multinational companies. A well-known example goes like this: 800 yuan is needed to produce a microwave oven in the US. Liang Qingde cooperated with multinational companies to move the production line to Galanz and produced it for 400 yuan. Liang Qingde used a week to complete the multinational companies' one-month order and used the rest of the time to produce his products.

Liang Qingde passed the baton to his son Liang Zhaoxian in 2000. Galanz has maintained its status as a private enterprise and is not listed. Liang Zhaoxian was awarded the title of Outstanding Entrepreneur of Guangdong province during the celebration of the 40th anniversary of reform and opening up.

Vanward and Lu Chuqi

Established in August 1993 and listed on the Shenzhen Stock Exchange in 2011, Guangdong Vanward New Electric and Gas is the leading manufacturer of gas water heaters, kitchen appliances and hot water systems in China. It has seven major production facilities in Shunde, Zhongshan, Gaoming and Hefei. The production facilities cover an area of over 1 million square metres. In 2017, its sales reached 6.5 billion yuan, and its profits amounted to 400 million yuan. Vanward gas water heaters rank first in China and second in the world; its kitchen appliances rank third in the country and second in the world.

The company is the pioneer and promoter of China's gas appliances development strategy. It has led or participated in the drafting and revision of national standards for gas water heaters, gas cookers and disinfection cabinets. It has obtained more than 1,300 patents and is the most patented company in China's gas appliances industry. Vanward has seven innovation platforms, such as 'National Enterprise Technology Centre', 'Clean Energy Academician Expert Workstation' and 'Postdoctoral Scientific Research Station'.

The founder of the company, Lu Chuqi, was born in 1949. At the age of 38, Lu Chuqi started his business after leaving his job as a technician.

The success story of Vanward is widely circulated in Shunde. Lu Chuqi was awarded the title of Outstanding Entrepreneur of Guangdong province during the celebration of the 40th anniversary of reform and opening up.

Keda and Bian Cheng

Keda Clean Energy was established in 1996 and listed on the stock market in 2002. It is a high-tech enterprise specialising in the production of large-scale processing equipment for ceramic stone and engaging in the planning and construction of ceramic stone production facilities. It has garnered the title of the 'Chinese Ceramic Machine'. The company's sales in 2017 were 5.73 billion yuan, and the profits were 479 million yuan. The company covers an area of about 705,000 square metres and employs more than 4,900 people. Among them, 30% are armed with high and intermediate academic qualifications. The company has recruited some of the country's well-known experts and professors in the stone industry.

In just 20 years, Keda Clean Energy has grown from a handicraft workshop to become the first in China and the second in the world in the ceramic machinery industry and has become a benchmark for Shunde's machinery and equipment industry. Since its establishment, the company has successfully developed China's first SML (H) 21/16 stone continuous mill, China's first SJS48 granite sand saw, China's first automatic deep osmosis vertical glue production line, China's first thin sheet (composite board) production line, China's first marble static pressure line saw, and so on. Keda's product technology level is at the forefront of its international peers. It is China's most professional and most comprehensive stone equipment manufacturing enterprise.

Keda's chairman, Bian Cheng, joined the company in 1998 and gradually established a scientific and efficient management system. He practices the concept of 'distributing money to entice people', and has successfully attracted a large number of outstanding talents from home and abroad to build Keda. He has effectively transformed the company from a single equipment supplier to an enterprise that supplies the complete range of ceramics technology and equipment. The company has played a key and leading role in the technological advancement of the ceramic machinery industry worldwide. Bian Cheng was awarded the title of Outstanding

Entrepreneur of Guangdong province during the celebration of the 40th anniversary of reform and opening up.

Conclusion

Entrepreneurship has played an important role in the economic development of Shunde, and it is difficult to appreciate the development of Shunde without understanding this. Shunde has produced and nurtured new entrepreneurs and enterprises throughout its history. Today, with China's economic transformation, innovation has become the main driving force for Shunde's economic development. In the process, Shunde will once again foster the growth of new entrepreneurs and businesses. The always thriving entrepreneurial community is the source of Shunde's economic life.

Part 3
Holistic Approach to Development: Social Reform Complements Economic Growth

Chapter 14

Shunde's City Governance

From 1978 to 2017, Shunde's nominal GDP increased by nearly 650 times from 480 million yuan to 301.6 billion yuan. Annual per capita GDP increased from 600 yuan to almost 120 thousand yuan, and annual per capita disposable income increased from 226 yuan to nearly 50 thousand yuan. The economic success brought substantial financial resources to support Shunde's accompanying urbanisation and enabled it to deal with inevitable urbanisation by-product problems in education, sanitation and healthcare, pollution, transportation, safety, and social stability. The buoyant economy provided a sound foundation for Shunde to implement a smooth urbanisation process.

Shunde's residential population increased from 780 thousand in 1978 to 2.61 million in 2017, and urban residents increased from 20% of the population to 98.6%. Based on population distribution, Shunde classifies as a highly urbanised area. The district experienced four phases of urbanisation since the country's opening up: village-based urbanisation in the 1980s, rural-urban integration in the 1990s, accelerating urbanisation in the 2000s and urban upgrading into the liveable city after 2010. Regardless of the period, Shunde has always initiated innovative governance policies based on economic and social situations of the time, and this holistic approach allowed it to avoid many urbanisation pitfalls. As the forerunner of China's market economy, Shunde's experience on urbanisation offers a lot of valuable lessons on how to integrate urban governance and economic development.

Urban governance is typically divided into hard and soft aspects. Hard aspects refer to physical infrastructures befitting a city such as environmental facilities, urban planning, transportation, communication and other domains, while soft elements include security and social governance. The physical infrastructure aspects of urban governance is elaborated in the article 'Urbanisation in Shunde', and therefore this article focuses more on the soft elements.

Hard aspect of urban governance

Emphasising proper planning and adopting the latest knowhow

The initial two phases of turning Shunde from a rural backwater to urbanised industrial city — village-based urbanisation in the 1980s and rural-urban integration in the 1990s — saw the proliferation of factories across the district. Inefficient land use and poorly planned construction work were unwanted by-products of the transformation. When the district entered the accelerating urbanisation phase at the turn of the century, the district government initiated a rationalisation process on urban development, and the movement picked up momentum. In 2018, the Shunde government announced its seven top priorities which included proper planning and adopting the latest knowhow on urbanisation, as well as transforming and revitalising decrepit and poorly planned industrial parks. It also announced that its top focus for the next three years is to transform 33.3 square kilometres of inefficient village-level industrial parks into new industrial zones. For more detailed information regarding the government's focus and transformation of the parks, please refer to the articles 'Shunde's Successful Reforms' and 'Shunde's Industrial Parks'.

Preserving the environment and building a liveable city

Familiar problems facing rapidly industrialised cities include the proliferation of poorly planned factories and extensive pollution problems. The same goes for Shunde. Shunde's initial industrialisation phase in the 20th century came at the tremendous expense of the environment as industries were highly polluting and energy inefficient. In 2002, the water quality index was at a dismal 0.28, and aquatic life in waterbodies was almost non-existent. The air pollution index was 0.69, average noise level was 55.4 decibels, and annual acid rain frequency was 56.3%.

In the early 2000s, the district government realised the extent of the environmental crisis and began a series of remedial efforts to mitigate the adverse effects of pollution. It introduced an industrial zoning policy and relocated factories to specific industrial zones to facilitate pollution treatment, implemented urban environmental management and industrial pollution prevention measures, and put in place water treatment measures. Rejuvenation works for old mulberry ponds and inland rivers also started. By 2014, a 24 kilometres waterfront greenbelt and a 118 kilometres green corridor were built along existing water and road infrastructure, and per capita park area of 19.2 square metres and urban centre green coverage ratio of 40% was achieved.

In 2013, Shunde started the national forest city project. Between 2011 and 2017, the district added green area and brought the total to 1,377.98 hectares, and green corridors totalled 470 kilometres. One hundred eighty-four new and rejuvenated parks covering 606.14 hectares were constructed, and per capita green park area was 22.39 square metres. The district's green coverage ratio was 42.21%; including rooftop vegetation, the green rate reached 43.9%.

In 2018, Shunde started the Greater Bay Area (GBA) forest city project. The project aims to increase afforestation area by 1,500 hectares by 2022 and increase forest coverage rate by 3.03% in urban areas.

At the moment, Shunde's environmental remediation focus is to upgrade village-level industrial parks.

Soft aspect of urban governance

Prioritising livelihood

As a forerunner in China's economic reform and foreign trade, Shunde realised the importance of having a harmonious industrial relationship between economic and social development at an early stage. A harmonious industrial relationship indirectly promotes economic growth, and a robust economy, in turn, supports a more generous social spending programme. Shunde captured the virtuous cycle on economic growth and social stability and was the first district in China to address employment, living condition and social security concerns of workers.

In 1984, Shunde launched the country's first social security reform. All employees in TVEs under its jurisdiction were enrolled in the new social security programme. Although the outcome of the reform was unsatisfactory in terms of actual coverage and implementation, the attempt provided valuable lessons for future social security reforms. A very important consequence of this reform was the public's confidence in support of planned economic reforms: the message of sharing the fruits of economic development and the presence of a caring government were embedded in people's mind. Public's scepticism toward reforms was lowered, and the forward-looking social security reform paved the way for the reform of enterprises in 1993. In each of Shunde's milestone that followed, the topic on social security and livelihood have featured strongly.

Shunde has been a strong advocate of the property rights reform since 1993. Although the reform affected the interest of almost everyone in the city, it was widely accepted and did not cause any large-scale social unrest because the presence of a multi-faceted social security system provided a safety net to the affected populace. The second social security reform was implemented in 1994 as a complementary policy to the property rights reform. It consolidated different social security programmes, centralised collection, management and implementation, and established the main framework of Shunde's and China's modern-day social security system.

The third social security reform occurred in 2000 and introduced unemployment insurance. It expanded the coverage of the social security system to virtually all sectors in the economy. In 2002, Shunde introduced the first 'social security card' in Guangdong province which complied with all rules and standards promulgated by the central government.

In recent years, Shunde has carried out the fourth social security reform by setting up a more comprehensive and multi-tiered system incorporating both rural and urban areas. The scheme succeeded to raise minimum benefit payments every year and expanded coverage for the elderly, orphans and disabled.

Education and medical care are key concerns of every individual and family, and have remained the top spending priorities of the government.

During the initial years following the 1978 reform, the government focused on providing basic education and held remedial classes to raise workers' general knowledge. Since 1980, vocational schools have also been built to train technical personnel for the then-nascent industrialised Shunde.

The 1980s target on rural-urban education integration was basically met by the 1990s, after which Shunde's emphasis shifted to providing quality education. In 1998, urban and rural graduates achieved comparable educational attainment. Primary school enrolment reached 99.96%, junior high school enrolment 99.65%, senior high school enrolment 52.13%, and vocational school enrolment 91.6%. In 2006, Shunde implemented a nine-year free compulsory education programme and provided free miscellaneous fees for indigent and deserving students. Primary and junior high school enrolments reached 100%, and senior high school enrolment reached 99.36%.

Shunde's education sector has three distinct features. The first is the provision of high-quality and readily accessible basic universal education so that every student has equal educational opportunities. The second is its responsiveness to the workforce requirement of the economy. For a long time, Shunde emphasised vocational education to churn out graduates that fill the industry's labour force requirement, and more recently, following the industrial upgrading requirement, the government partnered with tertiary institutions to build research institutes and provide higher calibre graduates for research and development work. The close alignment between education and economic development not only facilitates industrial upgrading; it also minimises employment mismatch between graduates and industry. The last feature is the wide variety of schools that cater to students from different backgrounds. There are schools that partner with overseas international schools, special schools for underprivileged children, and private schools at various levels catered to particular needs. The provision of high-quality education nurtured qualified technical workers and is also a compelling reason for migrant families to settle in Shunde. For more information, please refer to the article 'Shunde's Education System'.

Shunde always keeps a closewatch on the development of its healthcare industry. Much support from the government, community and Shunde natives residing in Hong Kong and Macau have been received, and the industry has been making considerable progress. Shunde pioneered an insurance system that covers both rural and urban residents; in 1984, it implemented basic medical insurance for workers, and in 1994 for registered urban residents. Part of the insurance premium is covered by the individual while the other is covered by the government and subsidies.

To adapt to increasingly multi-faceted and diversified medical and healthcare needs, Shunde launched a healthcare institutional reform in 2009. A 3-tier grading system (primary, secondary, tertiary) was introduced in 2011, whereby hospitals are classified based on the number of beds they can accommodate and the type of services they provide. The more comprehensive services the hospital offered, the higher likelihood it will be called a tertiary hospital. Shunde's hospitals all strived to optimise resource allocation and improved their services to attain a high ranking (A, 2A or 3A). The Number 1 District Hospital, as well as the women and children's hospital, became the first two tertiary 3A hospitals in the district, and all its towns have 2A secondary hospitals (most village hospitals were primary hospitals offering limited service). At the same time, Shunde carried out its comprehensive healthcare reform and set up high-quality, standardised, community-based primary healthcare centres in ten towns (streets), and most of Shunde residents could reach a community health care centre within 15 minutes. With the promotion of family doctors, the government provided 14 free primary healthcare services such as health record management, health education, vaccination, maternal health check and other healthcare services. Accessibility to healthcare facilities improved vastly over the years.

Improving the livelihood of the people has always been the foremost consideration of the Shunde government. The government realised early on that livelihood holds the key to social stability in an era of rapid economic change, and that the only way for the economy to develop and for reforms to be accepted is when people are content with their situation. More than 70% of the government's annual fiscal expenditure goes to livelihood enhancement spending. The spending included physical infrastructure building as well as education and healthcare spending, which enhances human capital. Prioritising livelihood is an innovative and unique approach to city governance in Shunde.

Equalising and standardising rural-urban public services

Shunde transformed from an agricultural-based county to an urbanised industrial city using a two-pronged approach. The first approach was through industrialisation, and the second through rural area reform. During this process, Shunde learnt valuable lessons on grassroots governance and carried out many innovative policies to manage social tensions arising from rapid urbanisation. Its success in standardising basic public services for urban and rural folks was an important milestone for urban governance.

In the 1980s, the household contract responsibility system allowed farmers to keep all the profit after paying a small rent to the village government. The move boosted the morale of the farmers. Shunde also benefited greatly from this system. To further increase land productivity, the government encouraged the formation of cooperatives that resembled modern corporations in the 1990s. This reform was first in China.

During the early 2000s, Shunde started to reform collective assets management system by solidifying equity and quantifying assets. The move achieved three effects. It promoted urbanisation and facilitated migration of villagers into the city as they were still allowed keep their share in the securitised cooperative. It boosted the morale of the farmers and encouraged hard work, and also reduced conflicts caused by distribution.

On the issue of livelihood service, the rural-urban difference over education and healthcare systems were eliminated in the 1990s. From 2004 onwards, Shunde implemented a unified household registration reform. This move was an important phase of urbanisation. In 2011, it started to construct administrative service centres across all villages to improve village-level public service provision, and by 2012 there were a total of 201 administrative service centres.

In recent years, Shunde has implemented measures to improve the provision of basic services and instituted boards of supervisors in rural areas. The board of supervisors has the right to monitor and discuss village affairs, and its establishment boosted grassroots self-governance and is a meaningful institutional innovation.

The rural reform in Shunde revolved around three main areas: finding the most suitable land contract management system, developing the rural economy, and promoting grassroots governance. The district has been successful in promoting the integration of rural residents into the market economy and establishing the governance structure that integrates rural and urban societies.

Integrating new citizens

The success that Shunde got to enjoy in the past is not just attributable to hardworking locals. It is also due to the diligence of migrant talents. In the 1990s, the Shunde government and its enterprises started to attract migrant talents to supplement its labour force. In 2005, the number of talents reached 162,400, and they represented 13.5% of Shunde's population. This talent density was much higher compared to the whole province and the country.

Economic development in the 1990s led to a wave of migrants entering Shunde. Many of them were of high calibre seeking to find opportunities in Shunde, and some were ordinary workers. However, the massive influx of new people led to security problems, which brought challenges to city governance. 2005 was a watershed period for Shunde to manage its migrant population. During that year, Shunde combined the public security, housing, family planning administrations into a three-tiered, integrated management body to serve migrant workers' housing needs. The three-tiers were on a district, town (street) and village (community) level. The goals of this single-agency approach were to strengthen the management of housing arrangements, minimise fraud and illegal activities and provide migrants with a peaceful environment to work in and promote people-oriented services like one-stop service, door-to-door service, health consultation, child vaccination and so on to the family of the migrants.

In 2010, Guangdong introduced a residence permit system to replace its old temporary system. The new permit could be used in the entire province and allows for the availment of many social services. In 2012, Shunde renamed 'mobile workers' as 'off-site employees', focusing on the ten areas of providing employment support, skills improvement, working environment, welfare protection, residential improvement, children education, management participation, rights protection, equal opportunity, and shared happiness. The government launched four projects for migrant workers and their family: provide migrants with similar social service as locals, promote the concept of home away from home, help them reach their aspiration, and provide care and affection. In 2014, Shunde renamed the migrant population as 'new citizens'. A points system was introduced whereby accumulation of specific points will grant them residency right and their children could enjoy same schooling privileges as a local born. Points comprised of four components: basic, bonus, special district-wide indicators, special indicators set by each town (street). Basic indicators include personal particulars, social insurance status and living condition. Bonus indicators include meeting the skill requirement in the labour market, government priority area, patent innovations and social contributions, science awards, family planning and projects participation. Each town (street) also has 20 points that can be separately awarded based on community requirement.

In the same year, Shunde established the New Shunde People Service Association to help new citizens participate in social governance. As of July 2018, 1.906 million migrants in Shunde with valid resident permits could enjoy 18 basic public service benefits provided by the government. In recent years, Shunde has focused on providing basic public service benefits for the migrant population, providing them with various services in the fields of healthcare, social security, and children's education.

Meeting different social service needs and promoting high-quality development in public service

Under the backdrop of a highly-dense urban population, many urban problems related to family, youth, elderly, neighbourhood and shortage of social services have become more critical compared to the past. In 2012, Shunde established the 'District Innovation Centre' whose goal is to use modern corporate management methods to improve public service deliveries, strengthen the government's ability to provide public service and extend services to every corner of society.

During the same year, Shunde began to build a three-tiered social service system in towns and villages. At the district level, the District Social Innovation Centre is committed to establishing an innovative public welfare support mechanism and nurturing social organisations, enterprises and talents to solve social problems. It also encourages the establishments of the Workers Association, Social Service Association, and other associations which aim to combine resources and promote self-governance. At the town (street) level, the establishment of unique social service centres, industrial park staff service centres, youth centres and other centres aim to support professional service organisations and link up talents, projects and resources. At the village (community) level, reliance is placed on the 201 welfare associations and 174 social worker service stations to direct professional services right to peoples' doorsteps. Services cover family, elderly and youth services, drug rehabilitation, and so on. As of 2018, the district has 1,820 social organisations. One hundred and seventeen of them have been awarded 3A grade, which is the most compared to other counties or districts in Guangdong province.

In response to the negative impacts brought by industrialisation and urbanisation, in particular the declining sense of belonging and involvement in societies, since 2013, a pilot project directed by the government was implemented to respond to community needs, resolve community issues, rebuild a sense of ownership, enrich community services, beautify community landscape and revitalise the economy. By end 2018, 17 community demonstration sites were identified to actively promote cohesiveness and inject vitality in the community, creating a new pattern of grassroots social governance.

In recent years, Shunde has introduced a smart administrative system that addresses consultation, appointment, evaluation and inquiry needs of the citizens. The scheme covers 75 administrative functions and is broadly categorised into government review and approval, non-government review and approval, and miscellaneous services. Functions included are in the areas of administration, transportation, social security, taxation, livelihood, healthcare, travel, and industry and commerce.

Increasing transparency in public policy implementation

In 2012, Shunde was the first county in Guangdong province to pioneer the participatory budget scheme whereby locals were given the chance to participate in the budget formulation process. The project increases public involvement in government decision-making, provides more avenue for the public to voice out their suggestions and gives them more authority to decide what they want. It is an innovative reform with regards to budget preparation and distribution. The change has gradually matured over the years; in addition to soliciting opinions online and conducting discussions which occurred in the early stage, current plans include on-site inspection, supervision and evaluation. One hundred twenty-seven projects from 60 organisations, with a budget of 5.38 billion yuan involved, went through this process within five years.

In 2019, the participatory budget programme conducted by Shunde Finance Bureau and Shunde city's website handled 39 projects with a total budget of 21.16 billion yuan. The number of projects and amount of budget involved was the highest recorded.

Conclusion

Shunde has accumulated a lot of valuable experiences in urban governance and improving people's livelihood. The expansion of social services to the basic unit of society and the move toward greater transparency in government spending and policies helped to gather public support for the district government, and fits the aspiration of this generation of young, urban talent to have greater participation in public affairs and clamour for more social services. The skilful combination of soft and hard approaches of city governance has increased satisfaction level and has given a sense of well-being. In the face of inter-city rivalry to attract investment and talents under the Greater Bay Area, Shunde's drive towards a liveable city is the right competitive strategy. The district is in an excellent position to be one of the competitive cities under the Greater Bay Area.

Chapter 15

Urbanisation in Shunde

Cities and villages are two distinct biospheres. They are very different, but there is an evolutionary relationship between the two because all cities evolved from town and villages. Before the Renaissance and industrial revolution eras, cities existed either as an administration centre or as the country's transportation hub. The technology was backward, and problems brought by a dense population, such as in public healthcare and sanitation, energy supply, pollution, transportation and livelihood could not be addressed adequately. As such, urban population was limited to only hundreds of thousands.

The problems associated with a dense population were solved as technologies evolved in the 19th and 20th century. Application of ever-advancing technology not only eradicated these problems, but the emergence of urban centres also created new demand for high-end service industries which in turn created new jobs. These new jobs helped to solve the redundant labour problem brought by the mechanisation in agriculture. The economic benefits brought by talent concentration and technology clusters in the urbanisation drive were significant. The city's past function as a political, administrative centre and transportation hub no longer strictly applied as economic and educational services became defining parameters of many new cities. In these cities, economic vibrancy became their reason to exist and grow.

The Industrial Revolution in the 19th century saw the emergence of many industrial cities in the west. Coal was the source of energy, and notions regarding environmental protection and social responsibility were weak. Urbanisation led to many problems in governance, healthcare, education, environment and transportation. Following the shift to a service-based economy and an increase in environmental awareness, many industrial cities leveraged on existing human capital and financial resources to successfully transform into modern, liveable cities and continued to grow. However, some cities were unable to make the transition and gradually declined. One of the most notable cities in this failing class is Detroit.

Each stage of Shunde's urbanisation is accompanied by Shunde's economic development. The urbanisation process has four phases: village-based urbanisation in the 1980s, integration of rural and urban areas in the 1990s, accelerating urbanisation in the 2000s, and urban upgrading into the liveable city from 2010 onwards.

The 1980s: Village based urbanisation led by village-led industrialisation

In the first ten years of China's opening up from 1978, Shunde pioneered the formation of the TVEs and the 'three-plus-one' cooperative trade model. The innate ambition and daring attitude of locals also led Shunde to pioneer the country's first attempt at industrialisation. During the initial ten years of the reform, TVEs emerged in every village. This industrialisation was driven by the proliferation of unplanned and poorly regulated factories. The development of TVEs played a crucial role in Shunde's rural urbanisation, and the image that Shunde carried at that time was that it was neither a village nor a town. Factories, rice fields and fish ponds interspersed with each other, farmers and factory workers lived next to each other, and town centres were scattered in the middle of the agricultural fields.

Due to its proximity to Hong Kong and Macau, Shunde developed an early awareness of urban planning. Following the opening up of China in 1978, Shunde formulated China's first county planning initiative — the 'Daliang Town 1979–1985 Municipal Plan'. In 1984, Shunde took the lead in establishing a special government agency responsible for urban planning and construction, the Urban and Rural Construction Committee. The committee unified all urban planning, land acquisition, fundraising and construction activities. It also rolled out the 'Daliang Town 1985–2006 Master Plan' which formulated the development of one town centre, two growth axis and three town clusters in Shunde.

Table 1. Shunde population

Year	GDP (million dollars)	Hukou population	Non-hukou population	Total residents	GDP/residents (yuan)	Disposable income per urban resident (yuan)	Disposable income per rural resident (yuan)
1978	475	781000					
1980	529	793384					
1985	1503	848000					
1990	4419	918000	55000	973000		3377	1854
1995	16960	1009000	279000	1288000			
2000	36459	1081000	614000	1695000	22213	14394	6646
2005	82512	1163000	792000	1955000			
2010	178917	1225000	1238000	2463000	74420	30618	12543
2015	258668	1284000	1251000	2535000			
2017	301591	1393000	1222000	2615000	116914	49881	31918

In the 1980s, the source of Shunde's industrial labour was mainly excess local farmers who became redundant due to privatisation-driven productivity improvements. There was little demand for migrant workers in the 1980s. However, this source of farmer surplus labour dried up following the rapid industrialisation in the 1980s, and by the 1990s, Shunde needed outside migrant workers to sustain the industrialisation drive. This influx of migrant workers negated the effectiveness of the city planning done earlier. The migrant wave can be seen in the non-*hukou* population number in Table 1.

The 1990s: Rural-urban integration

In 1992, Shunde's administrative status elevated from a county to a city. It was later selected as 'Guangdong Province Comprehensive Reform Experimental City' and 'Urbanisation Pilot City'. The designations allowed Shunde to start a comprehensive reform which focused on government administrative reform and property rights reform. As part of the administrative reform, Shunde also pushed for rural and urban integration.

Following the implementation of the property rights reform, many TVEs were transformed into modern enterprises. Vitality was injected into these newly privatised businesses. The reform also solved the financial problems plaguing many TVEs as well as the problems faced by local village and town government sponsors, which was TVEs binge-borrowed to fund their insatiable investment appetite and that their management may siphoned out enterprise profit for private gain while leaving all liabilities to the sponsoring local government. After the reform, Shunde's initial 'three-plus-one' cooperative trade model was transformed into a higher level of industrialisation. Shunde's manufacturers became independent exporters who did not rely on outside technology and consigned raw materials.

The government's fiscal improvement following the property rights reform accelerated Shunde's urbanisation process as Shunde started to build a city centre area and focused on transforming the earlier mixture of industrial and residential areas. The move to disaggregate the factories area from residential areas began in early 1990s. In 1993, Shunde began the specialised industrial township programme to consolidate industries to achieve economies of scale and improve the living environment.

By the end of 1998, Shunde had a developed urban area of 63.52 square kilometres (70% more than in 1991), and the city had built an infrastructure of more than 12 billion yuan since 1978. Some residential areas with modern planning, novel design and comprehensive modern facilities were built, and living conditions improved significantly. For the first time, galleries, gardens and beautiful landscape filled the city. This period also saw Shunde standardising urban management. Orderliness, cleanliness and beauty of the urban environment became apparent. Shunde became a unique city which combined Lingnan rural and urban cultures.

However, rural-urban integration exposed two vital problems. The first problem was on industrial dispersion. Shunde had more than 200 industrial zones of varying sizes and location, the land utilisation rate was low, and a large number of industrial estates made central planning difficult. It was challenging to build a large-scale industrial zone, and this limited industrial upgrading and enterprise development. The second problem was that the city centre was not well developed. Although the development plan called for a prominent city centre, progress on the ground reflected a township image than a city centre image. Individual buildings were beautiful, but on aggregate they looked uncoordinated, infrastructure construction was backward, and small sidewalk stores dominated the landscape instead of large retail malls.

In 1999, Shunde's non-agricultural population accounted for 32.7% of the total population. Shunde itself identified mostly as a blend of a rural-and-urban-integrated minor city on the way to becoming a modern city.

The 2000s: Accelerating urbanisation

Shunde's economy continued to grow fast at the turn of the century. In 2000, it was declared as the first pilot city in Guangdong province to have achieved modern urbanisation. For four consecutive years (2000 to 2003), Shunde ranked first in the top 100 counties in China, and in 2006 its GDP went over 100 billion yuan. It was the first county-level city to achieve that level of economic output.

With the support of a strong economy, Shunde regarded urbanisation as a key indicator of modernisation. In 2000, Rongqi and Guizhou merged to become Ronggui Town, and later Daliang and Desheng merged to become the new Daliang Town. The proportion of the urban population in Shunde reached 58.4% in 2003, 14 years ahead of the 58.6% national average in 2017.

In 2002, Shunde became a district under Foshan city. As a result, Shunde's urbanisation plan was absorbed into Foshan's overall urbanisation development, and Shunde moved to a phase of rapid urbanisation. The city centre, with over one million residents from Daliang, Ronggui and Lunjiao, emerged by 2008. Public facilities like an administrative service centre, performing arts centre, library, Desheng Plaza and Shunfengshan Park were built, forming a new city centre. At the same time, Shunde improved public facilities for Beijiao, Lecong, Chencun, Longjiang and other towns, accelerating the level of urbanisation.

In 2009 the Shunde district's Development Planning and Statistics Bureau was formed. The bureau approved a plan formulated by urban experts — the Foshan City Shunde District Master Plan (2009–2020) — and Shunde decided to work on integrating then isolated towns to a unified metropolitan. Henceforth, urban planning was conducted on a district level and not just on township level. The plan to eliminate town development silos was a significant step in the continuing urbanisation drive. The master plan also envisioned Shunde to become a key player in the Guangzhou-Foshan greater metropolitan area.

Figure 1. Shunfengshan Park

However, urban and rural development in Shunde during the 2000s remained uneven. Most of the towns at the district were not able to deliver public services expected of a modern urban area and infrastructure remained relatively backward. Progress in industrial upgrading, regional integration and coordinated development also continued slow.

The 2010s onwards: Urban upgrading into a liveable city

In 2010, Shunde was assigned the special status of a city district directly under provincial government supervision in the areas of economic and fiscal management, social and cultural affairs. The expanded scope of power provided the right conditions for urban upgrading.

As the focus of Shunde's industries shifted towards high-tech manufacturing, attracting high-calibre migrants to transform the economy became a priority. Upgrading the district into a liveable city became key to attracting talents and also an important consideration in terms of urbanisation. The district accelerated environmental improvement works to rectify earlier legacy issues of pollution and coordinated city planning.

The focus of the 2011 urban upgrading programme shifted from the earlier city-economy approach to city-economy-modern living approach.

The additional consideration of modern living into city planning increased the importance of creating a conducive living environment, and as a result, city planning integrated more greenery, leisure and education facilities. The change emphasised the needs to meet the aspirations of the high-end population. In 2017, Shunde became a highly urbanised area where proportion of urban residents reached 98.6%. Many towns and streets in the district also had their unique development theme.

In 2011, Shunde started the implementation of a three-year urban upgrading plan (2012–2014). The main aim of the project was to make the district more liveable by improving Shunde's urban clusters, living environment, public infrastructures and using smart urban technology, and so on. After the three-year upgrade, Shunde pushed out another two-year extension plan (2015–2016) to improve the results of the original plan. In 2016, the five-year urban upgrading plan met its set target.

In 2011, Shunde also pioneered the construction of themed towns. Beijiao was assigned as the role of a representative town for upgrading. In 2016 and 2017 respectively, Beijiao and Lecong won the recognition of national-level special themed towns.

High-quality developments

On January 2018, Shunde implemented a new three-year action plan to strengthen the city centre. The project consists of developing a modern, vibrant and liveable city centre with 1.5 million people and using this to lead the pack of special, uniquely-themed towns.

Shunde's city upgrade programme is currently proceeding smoothly. In terms of transportation, a network within and outside of Shunde have already been formed. The network follows a '30:15' guideline, whereby 30 refers to the 30-minute driving time taken from one town to the other within Shunde, and 15 refers to the 15-minute driving time from any town to the nearest expressway. The current Shunde transport network will complement the transportation plan of the Greater Bay Area, whose transportation network envisions a one-hour travel time by either high-speed train, car or water transport between two city centres of the eleven component cities. For more information, please refer to the article 'Shunde: A General Introduction'.

Table 2. Unique development theme and industrial clusters of each town/street in Shunde

Town/ street	Area (sq km)	Household population (2017)	Development theme for town/street	Signature industrial clusters
Daliang	80.29	252431	Excellent Daliang	Trade
Ronggui	80.27	226212	Innovative Ronggui	Home appliances, machinery and equipment
Leliu	90.78	124495	Ingenuine Leliu	Home appliances, automobile parts, hardware, lighting
Lunjiao	59.30	94128	Liveable Lunjiao	Jewellery, woodwork machinery
Xingtan	121.98	139401	Water town Xingtan	Hardware, home appliances, new materials
Beijiao	92.11	142514	Charismatic Beijiao	Home appliances manufacturing
Lecong	77.85	120668	Creative Lecong	Plastics trading, furniture trading, steel
Longjiang	73.85	109179	Wisdom Longjiang	Furniture manufacturing, plastic product manufacturing
Junan	79.45	93946	Beautiful Junan	Jeans and clothing
Chencun	50.70	89697	Green Chencun	Machinery, flowers industry
	806.57	1392671		

Shunde is currently building two city centres: Shunde New City and Foshan New City. These two centres are designed to provide all amenities present in a modern liveable city. Ten major projects including traffic engineering, science museum, the renovation project of Guipan river system, brightening and beautifying the city centre, the Desheng Sports Centre, half marathon race track, transforming the cultural blocks, Desheng Business District and the Shunde Tower are also underway to improve Shunde's city liveability.

In terms of transforming old industrial estates, Shunde's current 205 villages house 382 small and often decrepit small village-level industrial parks. These legacy industrial parks cover nearly 9,000 hectares and accounts for 70% of industrial land in operation, and the plan is to transform 3,300 hectares of these parks to modern ones from 2018 to 2020. As Shunde sets new industrial zone clusters, the redevelopment of the old village-level industrial estates into modern industrial parks will likely take some time.

Figure 2. Shunde is a pioneering model city for eco-friendly development

The project will also consider the impact on employment and the government's overall industrial upgrading plan. For more information, refer to the article 'Shunde's Industrial Parks'.

In terms of environmental control, the Ministry of Ecology and Environment announced in 2018 that Shunde is a pioneering model city for eco-friendly development. In recent years, Shunde has made progress in improving air, water and soil pollution. With the exception of urban sewage treatment rate (95.3%) and village environmental development rate (80.8%), Shunde achieved all the environmental improvement targets it set in 2018. Treatment of sewage, garbage and hazardous waste are the foci of future treatments. Water pollution treatment is also a focus, and the quality of water has been improving every year.

Conclusion

Shunde's urbanisation process has always been linked to its economic development. This approach ensures good coordination between the two factors and avoids the situation where any medium- to long-term urbanisation plan implementation is derailed by sustainability problems that might arise from unexpected medium or long-term economic turbulence. It also ensures that urbanisation does not negatively affect economic development or create employment and social instability. The holistic approach to urbanisation and economic growth is an experience that Shunde can share with other Chinese cities.

The current drive towards a liveable city is proceeding well and is very promising. The GBA plan will affect the urbanisation process of the district. Shunde has the foundation for striding towards a brand new modern city and the ability to meet new challenges in the future.

Chapter 16

Shunde's Talent Management

Shunde used to be a typical agriculture-based county. Fish pond and sugar cane fields dominated the landscape, and although Shunde was wealthier than other areas in the country, it was still a rural backwater. In 1978, the total industrial and agricultural output value of the county was 847 million yuan. The annual per capita disposable income of farmers, who accounted for more than 80% of the population, was only 100 yuan. The economic foundation was weak, industry was limited to necessary agricultural processing and primary machinery industry serving the agricultural sector, and there was little talent in other manufacturing industries (for more information, refer to 'Shunde and the World Economy'). Shunde today, however, has risen to become a famous industrial city in Southern China. Its home appliances and machinery industries are renowned all over the country. In 2017, Shunde's total GDP exceeded 300 billion yuan, and annual per capita disposable income of urban and rural residents reached 50,000 yuan and close to 32,000 yuan respectively. The phenomenal transformation witnessed in the past 40 years is closely related to the open and innovative talent policies implemented.

Background to Shunde's enterprises and talent policies

Shunde's economic achievement in the 1980s was attributable to the development of TVEs, which were businesses started by local enterprising cadets and nominally owned by the towns and villages where they are based. TVEs were behind in technology and lacked money. Their survival was contingent on using entrepreneurs' keen business sense to exploit market gaps. The TVEs' competitive advantage in the market was based on productivity and keen market sense, as they believed in a technology-driven competitive advantage.

Being driven by this market-oriented mechanism, the desire to move up the technology ladder, tap new technology to develop new products, improve product quality and expand market share became second nature to the TVEs.

Technology-driven transformation needs technology talents to carry out its daunting tasks. In the 1980s, Shunde's government and entrepreneurs adopted a two-pronged approach to cultivate talents. The first approach was to attract technically-competent migrants. By 1991, almost 10,000 migrant engineers and technicians moved to work at Shunde, providing a robust human resource base for Shunde manufacturing enterprises to expand. The second approach was to nurture local talents through education and training through a variety of ways and channels. During the 1980s, there were only 5,526 polytechnic students with formal qualifications. In 1980, the whole county had close to 2,000 enterprises, yet there were only 14 university-level degree holders and 37 technical school graduates. There were no qualified engineers. In 1990, the number of degree holders (including teachers and doctors) increased to 15,260, an increase of 34.7 times compared to 428 in 1982. Most of these people worked in TVEs in the manufacturing sector.

Shunde's shortage of engineering talent was so acute in the 1980s that it gave rise to the phenomenon 'Saturday Engineer'. During the weekend, many engineers from SOEs at the neighbouring Guangzhou city would moonlight at budding start-up TVEs in Shunde to serve as their technical advisor.

In 1987, the Shunde government introduced four policies that proved transformational to Shunde's economic development. The measures, which were related to personnel management, institutional setup, staff compensation and product pricing, cut down government interference and granted more autonomy for enterprises to run their businesses. This company rights devolution not only matched businesses' workforce requirements to their growth requirement, giving companies much more flexibility to recruit talent, it also allowed differential compensation schemes to be implemented based on an individual's contribution to corporate growth, enticing the nominally government-owned TVEs to transform themselves into fully market-oriented businesses. The policies enabled enterprises to be better placed in giving tangible and intangible support to encourage innovation and raise morale. This reform was revolutionary in China, and many cities and towns followed it.

By 1992, Shunde had already established a relatively modern and robust industrial sector. Industrial output reached 16.01 billion yuan in 1991, more than 12 times compared to 1978. The entire county had 18 and 262 enterprises with annual sales of over one billion yuan and one hundred million yuan respectively. 25% of China's electric fans, rice cookers and water heaters came from Shunde, and Rongsheng's refrigerator sales ranked first in China. At that time, Shunde's enterprises churned out a new product every two days, and Shunde became the country's home appliances innovation centre and a famous manufacturing city in Southern China.

In 1992, Shunde implemented another transformational reform. The comprehensive administrative reform focused primarily on property rights reforms of the TVEs. It encouraged companies to orientate their entire operation towards market discipline and put firm competitiveness as the core competitive advantage. As a result, a solid foundation for the economy was built.

A market-based economy requires enterprises to make business decisions based on market signals and needs. Investment decisions should be based on market demand, technology investments made based on these decisions, and relevant technical personnel hired to use these technologies. A famous catchphrase among Shunde entrepreneurs in the 1980s and 1990s was 'use the money to attract talent, and use the talent to earn money'. Shunde entrepreneurs believed that the market was the key driver for technological innovation and that speedy adoption of science and technology was the key to a vibrant company. They also believed that technology is useful and meaningful only when it can translate into new products in the market. Increasing product variation and improving product quality became the primary goal, and engineers and technicians became the backbone of each company. This Shunde growth model brought positive results for companies that lacked talent and was financially weak.

Many companies in Shunde had an internal ranking and promotion system that was not based on the government certification system but instead based on company requirement and performance. This merit-based system rewarded talents and encouraged them to work even harder for their company's future.

As early as the 1980s, the Shunde government played a crucial role in bringing in talent migrants. It proactively investigated businesses' human resources requirements and instituted measures to attract migrant talents from other parts of China to resettle at the city. Operating within the migration policy frameworks of the central and provincial governments, the Shunde government was able to attract the migrants needed for its economy, help them settle, enrol their children to school, provide medical care and assist in helping their spouse find a job. The conducive environment designed to accommodate migrant talent was the main reason why the plan was successful.

Shunde's economic transformation and the change in talent demand

In the last century, Shunde's manufacturing sector growth depended on increasing input and business size to drive economies of scale and gain market share. However, continuous economic development resulted in higher labour and production costs that cut its competitive advantage compared to neighbouring areas. There was a need to adopt a different growth strategy and transform its industries to become highly value-added. The new policy was to strengthen competitive advantages of existing industries and develop new high value-added sectors.

Shunde's earlier migrant talent attraction drive concentrated on attracting engineers and technicians to run operations and improve efficiency. For Shunde to develop new high value-added industries, talents in new technology and higher education must be brought in to jumpstart the more innovative economy. As a result, the Shunde government expanded its successful two-pronged talent attraction policy. On the one hand, it created more ways and channels to nurture local high-end talents (for more information, refer to 'Shunde's Education System'), and on the other it added more incentives to support the resettlement of high-end migrant talents.

At the end of 2011, Shunde held its first talent attraction conference. The 'Talent driven growth strategy' was officially launched, and the '1 + 10' talent policy introduced. The '1' referred to the policy document aimed to accelerate the talent building and attraction strategy (now known as the 'talent drive decision'), and the '10' referred to 10 specific policies that supported this decision. The introduction of the strategy and plans allowed Shunde to attract a fresh wave of people whose skills were needed for Shunde's new economic development.

In 2015, Shunde's economic and industrial transformation required even more high-calibre talents. Shunde government released an updated set of 30 policies to attract talent. The new policies address issues ranging from drawing and nurturing talents and talent teams to building a supporting system for migrant talent start-ups. They aim to provide a more comprehensive support system for new talents in all aspects of their life. Compared to previous talent policies which aimed only to make settling down more manageable, the new policies include helping them set up their business in Shunde.

Currently only less than half of the population in Shunde are native Shunde locals; more than half are 'New Shunde people' who come from other regions in the country or other countries. Shunde has been successful in integrating migrants as one of their own, and this reflects Shunde's open and inclusive culture. The harmonious relationship enjoyed between locals and non-locals is the reason why Shunde remains bustling and innovative. Shunde has managed to retain its own culture while at the same time integrating the culture of others, and this inclusiveness makes Shunde's new policy of attracting migrant talents even more enticing.

Attracting talents amid competition

In recent years, Shunde put forward a set of standards to identify talents in education, industries, and medical and healthcare system. In these three designated priority areas, talents are divided into six groups. Assessment of talents who are eligible for further incentives is based on professional qualification and not on geographical, racial or other irrelevant factors. Past awards and achievements, job description as well as company-based positions and academic qualifications provided the information needed for incentive provision. Presently, Shunde has introduced a series of talent policies for migration and housing, enrolment to school (for their children) and other matters. Implementation of these policies is straight-forward. After the strict qualification verification, migrant talents will enjoy all incentives accorded for their moving to Shunde, and a migrant talent privilege card will be given to them to facilitate their enjoyment of all special privileges in financial and public services.

In 2017, some cities began to adopt similar incentive policies to attract high-end migrant talents. However, even with more intense competition for talents, Shunde still enjoys an edge due to its more experienced execution. The introduction of the 2018 affordable housing scheme, for instance, demonstrates its ability to move one-step ahead over other cities.

Shunde has an active talent-attraction principle of 'settle in Shunde, serve Shunde, and contribute to Shunde'. However, for high-end migrant talents deemed critical to Shunde's economic development, the residency requirement is handled with flexibility. It has never demanded the talents to serve and contribute to Shunde by leaving their original work unit and moving to Shunde. It just devises some means for the talent to contribute to the district through various creative schemes. This flexibility in attracting talent is a hallmark of Shunde.

Conclusion

Shunde today faces both opportunities and challenges from industrial upgrading and the formation of the Greater Bay Area. Attracting high-calibre talent is critical in meeting the challenges and tapping the opportunities. The cities of the Greater Bay Area are located at different positions of the smiling curve, complementing one another. The Greater Bay Area itself is an important manufacturing hub for China and the world due to its strong industry foundation and complete supply chain. Hong Kong provides excellent modern world-class service when it comes to logistics, finance and professional service. Relatively backward cities in the Greater Bay Area can make use of the arrangement to attract thriving industries from developed areas, while developed regions can transfer its low value-added activities to cheaper nearby locations in the Greater Bay Area to maintain the competitiveness of its companies and concentrate on developing high-end industries.

Today, Shunde is facing the opportunities and pressures of industrial upgrading and integration of the Greater Bay Area, which requires more talent input. It is inevitable that the economic performances of cities in the Greater Bay Area will differ, but Shunde's performance relative to others will depend on the rate of inflow of high-calibre talents. Its longstanding inclusive and supportive philosophy and policies for migrant talents will surely give it a competitive edge.

Chapter 17

Shunde's Education System

Shunde has always placed the utmost importance on education. Historically, Shunde had given birth to four top scholars in the imperial examinations. The advent of the knowledge economy has made human resource a core element of reform and development, and education is the foundation for cultivating talents. Basic education as a free public good is also responsible for achieving social equity, developing modern citizens and maintaining social stability. Over the years, Shunde has adhered to the principle of 'standards, service, and support' and has established a complete education system covering pre-school education, basic education, higher education, vocational education, adult education, community education, and special education. The system has given local residents an excellent educational foundation and has also provided a large number of talents for regional economic development. A development strategy of 'opening and innovating' has produced many educational milestones in primary education, vocational education, high-end private education, higher education, special education and other aspects. This article will explore how Shunde creates talents from its resident pool.

An overview of Shunde's education system

In the 1990s, Shunde, as a pilot reform city of Guangdong province, carried out a series of changes in the field of education. It established a multi-prong investment mechanism, and the education sector has since been significantly developed. Today, Shunde is recognised as a strong education area in

Guangdong province, an advanced area for promoting education modernisation in Guangdong province, and an advanced area for promoting the balanced development of compulsory education throughout the country. It has established a comprehensive and balanced modern education system ranging from pre-school education, basic education, vocational education, adult education, community education, special education and higher education. There are 228 elementary and middle schools in Shunde (including 205 public schools and 23 private schools), of which 192 are compulsory education schools (including 17 private schools), 22 are high schools (including six private schools), and 13 are vocational and technical schools. There are two colleges and universities, and one special education school. The pathways between the different schools are inter-connected and meet the educational needs of society.

Shunde's education development has always been at the forefront of the country. In the 1980s and 1990s, Shunde's elementary and higher education became universal. Today, the enrollment rates in kindergardens, elementary schools and middle schools are as high as 100%, and high schools' enrollment rate is 99.36%. The elementary and middle school enrollment rates of the disabled and intellectually disabled groups also reached 100%. In recent years, Shunde has been recognised many times as an advanced area in education modernisation and balanced development at the provincial and national levels, and is selected as a pilot unit for education reform.

In 2016, Shunde launched a comprehensive reform in education, focusing on the transformation of the school management system, management mechanism, human development and education branding. Efforts were made in aspects such as reforming the education management system, building a modern school system, innovating the talent training mode, and promoting professional growth of teachers. The aims were to boost the vitality of Shunde's educational development, form a Shunde education brand, meet the talent needs of Shunde's economic and social development and meet the increasingly diverse educational needs of the citizens.

According to 'Shunde District Education Development 13th Five-Year Plan', 'Shunde District High School Education Development Strategy Implementation Plan (2017–2021)', 'Shunde District Compulsory Education Construction Plan for the Next Five Years' and other educational programmes, the Shunde District Government will promote some benchmark schools, including two leading high schools, four major vocational education groups, and 6–8 high-quality compulsory education schools, to build a balanced, high-quality, diverse and distinctive system.

Basic education: Balanced development, fruitful results

As early as 2004, all ten towns (streets) in Shunde have become models of strong education to be emulated by other cities and towns in Guangdong. In 2008, under the continuous and unremitting effort of the Education Department, unified education standards and compulsory education were achieved through a two-prong approach of using hardware and software. In 2009, Shunde attained basic education for all urban and rural areas. All of the compulsory education schools in Shunde have become standardised schools, as measured by the compulsory education criteria of Guangdong province. In terms of quantity, there are 213 ordinary elementary and middle schools in Shunde, including 190 public schools and 23 private schools with more than 300,000 students. In terms of quality, the inter-school equilibrium coefficient of Shunde is the lowest in the five districts of Foshan, while its equilibrium degree is the highest in the five districts. The enrollment rate of junior high school students is 100%, the enrollment rate of elementary school students is also 100%, and the nine-year compulsory education coverage rate is 100%.

Economic development has continuously enhanced the attractiveness of Shunde to migrant workers. The rapidly increasing population has generated huge demand for social services, which have brought significant challenges to the local government. To this end, the Shunde District Education Department has on the one hand increased investment in education, such as increasing the supply of basic education resources. On the other hand, according to the principles of 'school classification' and 'student stratification', Shunde's local schools are divided into 'public' and 'private' schools to coordinate and integrate educational resources. Public schools are mainly for students with household registration in Shunde. Private schools have no such restrictions and are open to the whole society. 'Stratification' refers to the division of students in Shunde into local and migrant students. Migrant students are further divided into priority and normal according to local policy preferences. Students with household registrations are enrolled in the nearest school, while the rest of the vacancies are then allocated accordingly to priority migrant students and normal migrant students. Also, the Shunde District Education Department strictly controls the age of enrollment for elementary and middle school students and implements an enrollment policy of batch and point system. In this way, the basic education needs of all social groups are realised, and there is a fair and equitable distribution of educational resources. The universal availability of good education solves the worries of high-level migrant talents and helps to keep them in Shunde.

In September 2018, with a total investment of 782 million yuan and a campus area of 79,738.43 square metres, the Beijing Normal University Liyun Experimental School was officially completed and started operations. As the first 'School-District Cooperation' in Shunde, it is a private school with an innovative nine-year system. It is not only a pioneer in the cooperation between Shunde District Government and Beijing Normal University but it is also a non-profit institution. The number of classes (the highest number in Shunde) includes 48 junior and senior high school classes and 36 elementary classes and there are 4020 vacancies, which greatly ease the difficulty of local students entering the school. Also, a convenient location, advanced teaching equipment and a beautiful natural environment, as well as a quality faculty team

Figure 1. Beijing Normal University Liyun Experimental School

(more than 88% of their teachers graduated from 'double-first class' universities and more than half of the teachers have postgraduate qualifications), is pioneering an advanced level in basic education in Shunde.

The New Fengsha Elementary School, located in the new city east of Shunde, will begin operations in September 2019. The campus covers an area of 32,000 square metres and can accommodate 2,700 students in 60 classes. As a complete elementary school, the school building, canteen, gymnasium (indoor basketball court), 300-metre circular runway, football field, badminton court, volleyball court and other living and learning facilities will provide students with a convenient living and learning environment.

The continuous expansion of the basic educational resources in Shunde not only meets the growing educational needs but also gradually improves the quality and level of education. The future looks rosy indeed!

Vocational education: Providing technical talents for Shunde's industries

Shunde's vocational education has an early start, and the system has been perfected to send a large number of workforce to the local industries every year. Among the 14 vocational and technical schools in the district, Shunde Polytechnic is the national benchmark higher vocational college. There are also 13 middle vocational schools, including three national model middle vocational schools, six national key vocational schools and four provincial key vocational schools.

With the continuous improvement of the level of economic development, the Shunde district government is re-examining the functional and developmental directions of Shunde's vocational education in combination with urban district planning, industrial layout characteristics and social development needs. It has implemented the reform of vocational education with group-based schools with Shunde characteristics.

The 'One School in One Town' policy is instituted, and four major vocational education groups with clear and differentiated training objectives are established. Under this group-based management, the vocational speciality has a total of 37 majors, such as the application and maintenance of robots, jewellery and jade processing and marketing, furniture design and production, and others, and the positioning of the vocational courses are highly

Figure 2. In June 2018, the Shunde Chef College was launched at Shunde Polytechnic

integrated with the local industries. Of these, students in 26 majors including jewellery, furniture, hotel management, e-commerce, auto repair and others, are seamlessly trained from middle to higher vocational schools. There are 11 colleges and universities in the province that offer higher-level vocational training. Students can also apply for the three-year school-enterprise integration programme, etc. The Shunde vocational education system has been well established with structural optimisation, distinctive features, outstanding brand and social appreciation.

In 2018, the four major vocational education groups in Shunde actively cooperated with local industries according to their own development objectives. The district established the Shunde Home Design Industry College, Lecong Furniture College, Shunde Smart Appliance Industry College, Shunde Chef College, Urban Rail Transit Industry College, Shunqi Catering Training Industry College, Zhongkai Automobile Industry College and Guangdong Light Industry Shunde Jewelry Industry College. This platform, combining industry and education, will train high-quality talents that meet the needs of modern industry.

In 2018, there were 8,136 middle-school vocational graduates in Shunde, of which 4,097 were enrolled into higher institutions, and 4,039 were employed. The employment rate was 100%, and 87.72% of the employed students got jobs in their field of study. Taking vocational education group

Figure 3. Students from Chencun Vocational and Technical College undergoing training at Keda Clean Energy

management as the starting point, Shunde has deepened the integration of industry and education, strengthened the connection between middle and high vocational schools, expanded international exchanges and cooperation. The vocational school system has also improved third-party evaluation and the evaluation mechanism, realised 'precise education, precise allotment' between vocational schools and enterprises, comprehensively enhanced economic and social development capabilities in the service economy, and improved the quality of personnel training.

Private education: Diversified and globalised

As public education resources are relatively limited, Shunde Government encourages the private sector to run educational institutions. The majority of the 23 private elementary and middle schools in Shunde are first-class schools in Guangdong province, providing about 49,000 vacancies for the whole district, helping to alleviate the shortage of public education resources.

Private schools such as Country Garden School and Desheng School have first-class teaching facilities and school buildings, as well as excellent faculty teams, and advanced teaching concepts. They are also active in multi-disciplinary exploration, such as in international exchanges and curriculum reforms. Also, the Shunde Private Education Association, established in 2004, has civil supervision power over private schools and it has played an active role in promoting and coordinating private school education standards and norms, sustaining development, and building a communication platform for private education.

Private education groups such as Country Garden School in Shunde have set up international classes for Hong Kong, Macau and Taiwan students, benchmarked themselves against international teaching modes and examination mechanisms, and trained international talents. Their excellent university enrollment rates have attracted children of high-level talents to enrol. Shunde Desheng School (International) has an international faculty and has two academic pathways (International Baccalaureate and China's National College Entrance Examination) for students. Besides regular academic programmes, students' holistic development and extra-curricular activities are also promoted.

Figure 4. Desheng School's leadership training camp

Special education: Inclusive education for all

The balance and inclusiveness of education are not only reflected in the number of people it accommodates, but also in the diversity of social groups. The children with disabilities group has long been in a weak position in society, especially in economically underdeveloped areas, and its basic right to education is often overlooked. The Shunde government has always attached great importance to the survival and development of this group, and the developed economy has given the district government sufficient financial power to promote the development of the special education project. Since the special education project started in the 1990s, Shunde has expanded and developed a comprehensive special education system from its many years of study, exploration and innovation.

On the one hand, the Shunde Education Department encourages children with disabilities to study in public schools and provides rehabilitation training and psychological counselling for disabled students through 'resource classrooms'. On the other hand, the special education schools utilise 'cloud platforms' such that it is convenient for students with limited mobility to receive rehabilitation training and education at home. At present, there are 342 students with disabilities in the compulsory education stage in Shunde, with 199 students attending classes and 155 students home-schooled.

Figure 5. Qizhi School participated in a football tournament in Guangzhou

It is worth mentioning that the Shunde government has invested a total of 56 million yuan since 1999 in the construction of Qizhi School. It is a comprehensive boarding school for special education students with nine years of compulsory education. The students are moderately retarded, and some are hearing impaired. With the goal of 'cultivating students to lead dignified lives in society', the school carries out rehabilitation training for students, cultivates students' independence and hone their survival skills with its varied and rich curriculum activities. The school ultimately wants its students to be self-sufficient and integrate into society. Qizhi School has a total of 434 vacancies annually for the whole district. However, due to its humanised education, professional faculty and pleasant environment, it attracts a large number of students from outside Shunde to apply for admission every year.

Higher education: Develop talents for high-end industries

After meeting the needs of basic education, developing a diversified private education, promoting a market-oriented vocational education, and focusing on special education, the Shunde district government is beginning to develop higher education by adhering to the principle of meeting industrial needs, with a high starting point and high standards. It has successively built the Shunde Campus of Southern Medical University and Sun Yat-Sen University and the Shunde Graduate School of Beijing University of Science and Technology, as well as various postgraduate education platforms, including the Guangdong Xi-an Jiaotong University Academy and the Guangdong Shunde Innovative Design Institute and so on.

At the institutional level, Shunde has set up a district-level graduate education development centre to coordinate the recruitment and training of graduate students in Shunde. The centre promotes graduate education policy research, support and plan major events, manage the funding of postgraduate education, synergise different innovation platforms, manage the internship activities of Tsinghua University postgraduates, jointly train postgraduate students and administer postgraduate education and high-end enterprise training. In 2012–2018, more than 3,700 graduate students were recruited and trained through full-time cooperative education, joint postgraduate training, doctoral students' internship programme, and on-the-job postgraduate

Figure 6. Shunde Graduate School of Beijing University of Science and Technology

education. Among them, a total of 259 students from Tsinghua University and Zhejiang University were recruited through the doctoral students' internship project to carry out scientific research in Shunde's enterprises and institutions to help them solve technical problems. Through cooperation with famous universities at home and abroad in programmes such as joint training, platform incubation and professional training, Shunde is paving the road for its residents to fulfil their dreams of attending university.

Reform direction: Integrating resources

As a prestigious school with a 100-year history, Shunde No. 1 High School is the benchmark for the local education sector. With the integration of resources and the cultivation of the concept of group-run education, Shunde No. 1 High School Education Group, comprising of the central campus, Shunde No. 1 High School Foreign Language School, Ronggui Experimental School, and Shunde No. 1 High School affiliated elementary school — New Deye School, was officially established in December 2018. It is an educational alliance that integrates quality education in elementary school, middle school and high school. Its goals are personnel training, curriculum construction, teacher training, middle school-high school through train, resource sharing, and quality improvement to create a first-class basic education platform.

Furthermore, Shunde No. 1 High School is cooperating with Beijing Normal University Liyun Experimental School to jointly set up an experimental through train programme for middle and high school students, to explore a new mechanism for cultivating top-end talents. Also, Shunde No. 1 High School and 16 junior high schools in Shunde have set up an education alliance after more than a year of development. The goal is to develop and train high-quality students for Shunde's local high schools. Currently, Shunde has established nearly 30 education groups after overcoming regional restrictions and they cover various sections such as vocational education, compulsory education, and early childhood education.

While creating their own characteristics, high schools are also actively collaborating with colleges and universities to make their school features align with the college entrance examination. Offerings such as 'gifted class', 'foreign language class', 'media class', 'information technology class' and 'scientific and technological innovation class' are aimed at cultivating students' talents and are personalised for students. In the 2018 college entrance examination, one student from Shunde was ranked top 20 in the province, and three students were ranked top 40 in the province. Seven students from

Figure 7. Shunde No. 1 High School

the Shunde Experimental High School arts programme were ranked top 100 in the province. The fruits of Shunde's educational reforms are beginning to emerge.

Conclusion

Developing quality education is an inherent requirement for Shunde's economic development and a core element and important support for Shunde's regional competitiveness. Shunde rises to the different challenges such as society's needs, people's livelihoods and the market economy, fosters strengths and circumvents weaknesses, and makes full use of its resources to create an education system that meets the needs of the local community and conforms to local economic development. Shunde's education system not only benefits people's livelihoods, enhances the quality of its citizens, promotes the construction of a harmonious society, accumulates talents and sustains the developmental momentum for economic development, but also injects a new impetus into Shunde's integration into the Guangdong-Hong Kong-Macau Greater Bay Area.

Part 4
Future of Shunde in the Changing World

Chapter 18

Shunde's Future

Among the more than 2,000 county-level administrative units in China, Shunde has grown from an agricultural county to a leading economic region and a pioneer in reform through reform, opening up, and economic growth. The amazing achievements in Shunde's reform and opening up have proved that 'development is the real deal'. Shunde people's daring attitude and no-nonsense approach are given full play under the reform and opening up. The long-term unwavering support and continuous implementation of the 'industrial district (county) policy' from all levels of society, from the government and enterprises to the masses, is the cornerstone of Shunde's economic success. (The article 'Shunde's Successful Reforms' analyses economic development through reform.)

The past successes of Shunde are cemented by the core policy of the district government — long-term economic development. Shunde's future will also focus on sustainable economic growth.

In 2018, the per capita output value of Shunde exceeded 120,000 yuan, twice the national average and matching the level of developed countries. In the past, the added value of traditional manufacturing production was not enough to support the needs of sustainable economic development. So, on the one hand, Shunde opened up high value-added emerging industries; on the other hand, it guided the transformation and upgrading of traditional manufacturing industries and increased the added value of their production (for details, see the article 'Shunde's Emerging Industries'.) Manufacturing is the backbone of Shunde's economy. Whether Shunde's manufacturing industry can smoothly transform into high value-added modern manufacturing is the key to Shunde's economic development. The economic challenges facing Shunde are also problems facing the entire Pearl River Delta manufacturing industry.

The central government officially established the Guangdong-Hong Kong-Macau Greater Bay Area Development Leading Group in 2018 to coordinate the development of the GBA. Subsequently, on February 18, 2019, the 'Guangdong-Hong Kong-Macau GBA Development Plan' was officially announced. It is announced that Zhuhai and Foshan will be the leaders to build an advanced equipment manufacturing industry belt on the west bank of the Pearl River.

The position of Foshan will attract the country's production resources to flow to the advanced equipment manufacturing industry in Foshan, and provide effective support for the transformation of Shunde into a modern industrial system. These national and regional initiatives will boost the future development of Shunde. (For more information on the development of Shunde in high-tech industries and advanced equipment manufacturing industries such as robots and automation industries, please refer to the article 'Shunde's Industrial Parks').

Bay area economy

Since the beginning of the maritime era, trade has gradually become an important part of global economic development and an important bridge for the economic development of countries and regions. The ports along the coastal regions have provided the transportation needs of the global economy. In today's global economic development, the place that can lead global technological innovation and resource allocation is the bay area with waterways connected to the harbour. The economic effect derived from the geographical location of the bay area is called the bay area economy. The bay area has become a significant growth pillar for world economic development and is also a new platform for international competitiveness, especially in innovation.

There are four major characteristics of a globally successful bay area:

1) The economy, society and culture are highly open and highly inclusive.
2) The economy is innovative and the business environment is supportive.

3) Effectively integrates production resources in the region and creates the effect of 1+1>2.
4) A highly liveable area with many high-end talents.

According to World Bank data, 60% of the world's major cities are located in bay areas; 60% of the total economic volume is concentrated in the bay area and its hinterland; 75% of the world's largest cities, 70% of industrial capital and population are concentrated in the region 100 kilometres from the coast. Hence, the bay area economy has become an important development area.

The three most famous bay areas in the world are the New York Bay Area, the San Francisco Bay Area and the Tokyo Bay Area. The Guangdong-Hong Kong-Macau GBA is China's first bay area and one of the world's four newest and largest bay areas.

In the three established major bay areas, the Tokyo Bay Area is an 'industry bay area' that gathers one-third of Japan's population, three-quarter of industrial output, six ports along the coast, and a throughput of over 500 million tons. It is Japan's largest industrial city group, international financial centre, transportation centre, trade centre and consumer centre. The Bay Area of New York is a model of the 'financial bay area'. The largest 500 companies in the United States and more than one-third of companies' headquarters are located in the Bay Area of New York. The Bay Area of New York is the world's financial centre, with its finance industry, luxury industry and urban culture having worldwide influence. The San Francisco Bay Area is a model of the 'technology bay area', boasting the world-renowned Silicon Valley and more than 20 well-known science and technology research universities, such as Stanford and the University of California at Berkeley. It is also home to the global headquarters of technology giants such as Google, Apple, Intel, Facebook, Tesla, Nvidia, Gilead, Uber, etc. The San Francisco Bay Area has a high-tech personnel population of more than two million and is a gathering place for technology elites around the world.

As early as 2006, the Chinese government carried out research on the coordinated development of urban and rural areas in the Pearl River Delta. In 2009, the 'Study on the Coordinated Development Planning of the Greater Pearl River Delta Urban Agglomeration' identified the development of the GBA as the focal point for establishing cross-border regional coordination. In March 2016, China's '13th Five-Year Plan' (2016–2020) proposed the concept of the Pearl River Delta urban agglomeration. In July 2017, 'Deepening Guangdong-Hong Kong-Macau Cooperation — Promoting GBA Construction Framework Agreement' was signed by the local governments.

The construction of the GBA was written into the 19th National Congress Report of the CPC in 2017 and the Prime Minister's Government Work Report of the 2018 National People's Congress. The construction of the GBA has been upgraded to national development strategy level. It is a benchmark for economic transformation and upgrading.

Compared with the three established bay areas in the world, the Guangdong-Hong Kong-Macau GBA has two special characteristics: diversity in social and economic systems and large economic differences in the GBA. These two characteristics bring opportunities and challenges to the GBA: opportunities for economic integration and challenges of institutional differences, but the overall outlook has more opportunities than challenges.

Table 1. Basic data of the world's four major bay areas in 2016

	Guangdong-Hong Kong-Macau GBA	Tokyo Bay Area	New York Bay Area	San Francisco Bay Area
Resident population (ten thousand)	6765	4383	2370	768
Land area (10,000 km2)	5.60	3.67	3.45	1.74
Total GDP (trillion US$)	1.38	1.86	1.83	0.82
Major industries	Technological innovations, Financial services,	Manufacturing, Wholesale and retail	Financial services, Real estate, Health care	Technological innovations, Professional services
Tertiary industry (%)	62.2	82.3%	89.4%	82.8%
Port container throughput (10,000 TEU)	6520	766	465	227
GDP per capita (million USD/km2)	24.6	50.68	53.0	47.2
GDP per capita (US$)	21764	42865	86094	98637

Guangdong-Hong Kong-Macau Greater Bay Area

On February 18, 2019, the central government officially announced the 'Guangdong-Hong Kong-Macau GBA Development Plan', and the plan established four key strategic positionings for the GBA: international technology centre with global influence, important support base for the Belt and Road Initiative, deep cooperation demonstration zone between Mainland and Guangdong-Hong Kong-Macau, quality space suitable for living, travel and work. We can see that the central government is determined to build the GBA into a globally successful bay area, and hopes to lead the Chinese economy to a higher level through the GBA.

The Guangdong-Hong Kong-Macau GBA refers to the urban agglomeration consisting of the two special administrative regions of Hong Kong and Macau, and Guangzhou, Shenzhen, Zhuhai, Foshan, Zhongshan, Dongguan, Zhaoqing, Jiangmen and Huizhou in Guangdong Province. In 2017, the 9 cities in the Pearl River Delta of the GBA accounted for 30% of Guangdong Province's land area, 56% of the population and 85% of the total economic output. The per capita GDP was 18,000 US dollars in 2017,

Figure 1. Guangdong-Hong Kong-Macau Greater Bay Area

Table 2. Basic data of the Guangdong-Hong Kong-Macau GBA in 2017

City/region	Population (million)	Area (square kilometre)	Gross production (100 million US$)	Per capita GDP (US$)	Production value per sq. km. (100 million US$)
Guangzhou	14.5	7434	3180	21952	0.44
Shenzhen	12.5	1997	3320	26509	1.66
Zhuhai	1.8	1732	380	21502	0.22
Dongguan	8.3	2460	1120	13452	0.46
Zhongshan	3.3	1784	510	15665	0.29
Foshan	7.7	3798	1410	18460	0.37
Huizhou	4.8	11347	570	11868	0.05
Jiangmen	4.6	9505	400	8729	0.04
Zhaoqing	4.1	14891	330	7914	0.02
GBA (excl. HK, Macau)	61.5	54948	11220	18243	0.20
Hong Kong	7.4	1050	3420	46115	3.25
Macau	0.7	30	500	77111	16.67
GBA (incl. HK, Macau)	69.6	56028	15140	21764	0.27
China	1386	9600000	122400	8827	

twice the per capita of 9,000 US dollars in Guangdong province. The nine cities in the GBA are the economic core of Guangdong province.

According to Table 2, the statistics of 2017 showed that the GDP of Hong Kong, Shenzhen and Guangzhou is more than 300 billion US dollars (2 trillion yuan). These three cities are the core, first-tier cities of GBA. The total economic output of 2 trillion yuan is the same as the GDP of a province in China. The per capita GDP also exceeds that of the Yangtze River Delta and Beijing-Tianjin-Hebei cities. The GDP of Foshan and Dongguan exceeds 100 billion US dollars (close to a trillion yuan).

Shunde in the GBA

The 'Guangdong-Hong Kong-Macau GBA Development Plan' clearly points to Zhuhai and Foshan being the leaders to build an advanced equipment manufacturing industry belt on the west bank of the Pearl River.

Foshan's position is in line with Shunde's current industrial structure and the development direction of the district government. Shunde is expected to become one of the important beneficiaries.

1) At present, Foshan's industrial output value is the highest among all cities in the GBA (except Shenzhen). In 2016, it reached 471.9 billion yuan, much higher than Dongguan's 287.8 billion yuan. The proportion of industrial output accounts for 59.2% of regional GDP and is much higher than the 55% achieved by other cities. One of the most important national policy goals of the GBA is to build an industrial system with international competitiveness. As the core industrial area of Foshan, Shunde will receive considerable support in the policy.
2) Shunde's manufacturing industry is currently semi-automated. The traditional assembly line workshops are first upgraded to smart manufacturing and becomes fully automated with industrial robots and machine tools. Shunde's investment in these fields is early, and its support for the robots and automation industry is better than other cities. Although the GBA planning is guided by the government, success requires the cooperation of industry and market. In this respect, Shunde has the conditions to ride on the GBA's plan to promote advanced manufacturing. (For Shunde's work in emerging industries and industrial upgrading, please refer to the two articles 'Shunde's Industrial Parks' and 'Shunde's Emerging Industries'.)
3) Shunde is already very strong in the parts and components chain of the home appliances and machinery industries. Now combined with the high-tech research of Shenzhen, as represented by the location of DJI drone production facilities in Shunde, it has proved that Shunde has a viable economic model. Shunde is an important manufacturing base. In recent years, it has paid special attention to the robots and automation industries. Shenzhen has the advantages of high-end manufacturing, information technology and technological innovations. Shunde and Shenzhen are one of the important illustrations of the complementarity of cities in the GBA.
4) Shunde's manufacturing industry is dominated by local private enterprises. They have the characteristics of high flexibility and strong market adaptability. Private enterprises account for more than 70% of China's

total technological innovations. Shunde has the inherent advantages in implementing the transformation of the manufacturing industry.

5) Many traditional industries in Shunde are faced with land and cost constraints. The economic structure in the GBA allows low value-added manufacturing to move to a lower tier and other cities and lets high value-added activities to stay in Shunde. The development will encourage the 'headquarters economy' that Shunde has promoted in recent years.

6) In recent years, Shunde has implemented a series of policies to attract talents. Population growth in Shunde is the fastest among the cities in the GBA. Many scholars believe that the key to the success or failure of the GBA is the in-flow of high-end talents. Shunde is a leader in this respect amongst the second- and third-tier cities. To attract talents, Shunde is committed to creating a quality urban environment that is suitable for living and working. (For Shunde's work in improving the urban environment, please refer to three articles: 'Urbanisation in Shunde', 'Shunde's City Governance' and 'Shunde's Successful Reforms'.)

7) Shunde is famous for being a reform pioneer and for being pro-business. In recent years, it has been focusing on creating a better environment (both hardware and software) for enterprise development. These two achievements have attracted many new investments into Shunde. Faced with the diversity of systems in the GBA, Shunde is strengthening international cooperation and openly encouraging local enterprises to go global. On the other hand, it will also continue to attract foreign investors and talents to Shunde. It will become the focus of attention of investors and high-end talents.

8) A series of reforms introduced by the Shunde district government in recent years, such as 'Technology Shunde' proposed in January 2018, is generally consistent with the GBA Development Plan. The district government will assist in promoting and executing the GBA plan. (For the Shunde district government's reform plan, please see the articles 'Shunde's Business Environment' and 'Shunde's Successful Reforms'.)

To secure a high-quality development

Today's Shunde has not yet changed from a resource-intensive, labour-intensive industry to a technology-based industry. Whether it is industrial structure, economic growth mode, urban construction, rural environment, etc., there is a gap between the requirements of the new era and Shunde's current situation. Shunde has a clear understanding of its development; it is determined to grasp the development opportunities of the GBA, complete the transformation of village-level industrial parks and focus on the high-quality development of the manufacturing industry. In turn, Shunde wants to become a standard-bearer in systemic reforms, smart manufacturing, innovative technologies, international cooperation and quality of life.

1) Reform of village-level industrial parks. At present, Shunde is implementing a village-level industrial park reconstruction plan. It is planning and constructing several 10,000-*mu* (a unit of area, =0.0667 hectares) modern industrial parks, integrating 20 modern industrial clusters (each with more than 3,000-*mu* land area), and building 30 eco-friendly and modern-themed industrial parks. These parks will form a village-level industrial park mode known to be 'government-led, market-oriented and professionally-operated'. It will attract investment capital to participate on a larger scale and comprehensively improve the management quality of the parks, such that an environment is created for high-quality development.

2) Actively develop 'Technology Shunde'. Shunde will use innovation as the driving force for high-quality development and build a new homeland of technological innovations and transformations. It will give play to the role of enterprise innovation and accelerate the improvement of innovation capabilities. Earmarking smart manufacturing as an important engine for high-quality development, Shunde will establish a manufacturing optimisation and upgrading model that integrates technology, design, finance, and industry. In about five years, the home appliances industry will be upgraded to smart home appliances industry and will become a world-class industrial cluster of 600 billion yuan. It will build a national first-class robot education, research and development, manufacturing and application base. It will also cultivate 100 benchmark enterprises specialising in smart manufacturing, and its smart manufacturing industry will be at the forefront of the province and the country.

3) Create a first-class business environment with internationalisation, rule of law and convenience. Shunde will continue to improve its business

environment in accordance with World Bank standards. It will strengthen the construction of the 'digital government' and explore the application of artificial intelligence in public policy formulation. It will accelerate the implementation of the '1121' reform for enterprise investment and construction projects. Shunde will further promote the establishment of a 'single window' for international trade and carry out pilot projects for cross-border e-commerce import and export businesses. It will establish a new market supervision model with credit as the core, build a sound credit information system, and build a brand of 'Shunde integrity'.

Conclusion

The Guangdong-Hong Kong-Macau Greater Bay Area Development Plan is a national economic development strategy formulated in response to regional economic development. The region has a huge integrated market, complementary urban advantages, mature innovation and technological research and development, strong industrial strength, and world-class transportation and logistics network. The synergy between the manufacturing industry and the service industry in the region will be strong support for the GBA to become one of the engines of China's economic development.

Although Shunde does not have the economic influence of Shenzhen, Hong Kong and Guangzhou, it has a wealth of experience in the formulation and execution of reform, a strong local entrepreneurial base, a deep understanding of the district's developmental positioning in the GBA and a good manufacturing base. Shunde has good potential to become a key player in the second tier area of the Greater Bay Area.

CPSIA information can be obtained
at www.ICGtesting.com
Printed in the USA
JSHW010708301119
2711JS00001B/5